Qumran: New Light on The New Testament

By James Beasley

Qumran: New Light on the New Testament

Published in the United States of America
Lulu Enterprises
860 Aviation Parkway Suite 300
Morrisville, North Carolina 27560
www.lulu.com

The cover is a facsimile of 4Q394, a portion of 4QMMT dated paleo-graphically to the mid-second century B.C.E.

ISBN 978-0-578-02927-6

Printed in the United States of America

Second Edition

6 5 4 3 2 1

Table of Contents

Acknowledgements

This project has been a group effort from the beginning. I owe the completion of this project to a number of friends including my Pastor and friend Brett Peterson who never ceased to give me encouragement. I told him that I wanted to make sure this project was "readable" for the general public and he dived right in to make sure I was on track.

I would also like to thank Sheldon and Susan Stern who read an earlier draft of this project and did a careful and thorough job of proof-reading. They were both very kind in their comments and suggestions. EunJoo Kim used her extensive knowledge of Hebrew and Aramaic to review an early draft and to help completely revamp my Hebrew table and transliterations. Ms. Kim diligently critiqued some of my conclusions, and I have incorporated some of her ideas where I thought appropriate. I will always be grateful for her help.

I also wish to thank the many readers at my church who gave me their input on the "readability" question. If this project is "readable" it is in large part because of them. Of course, any mistakes that remain are mine alone. Finally, I wish to thank my wife, Chris, who gave me my space at the computer to hash out this project. I love you.

December 31, 2005

This second edition includes some revision and corrections of the first edition, along with the inclusion of a new chapter on Angels. I want to dedicate this second edition to my family at Ocean Hills Church which has been so supportive to me over the last year and one half. I hope my readers will find this edition more informative and enjoyable to read. It was certainly informative and enjoyable for me to write.

June 11, 2009
Jim Beasley

Definition of Terms

BAG is an acronym for "A Greek-English Lexicon of the New Testament." The full citation of the text is as follows: Arndt, William F. and F. Wilbur Gingrich. *A Greek-English Lexicon of the New Testament and Other Early Christian Literature.* Chicago: University of Chicago Press, 1957.

BDB is an acronym for "Brown, Driver, and Briggs." The full citation of the text is as follows: Brown, Francis, S. R. Driver, and Charles A Briggs. *A Hebrew and English Lexicon of the Old Testament.* Based on the Lexicon of William Gesenius as translated by Edward Robison. Oxford: Claredon Press, 1978.

NIDNTT is an acronym for "The New International Dictionary of New Testament Theology." The complete citation is as follows: Brown, Colin. General Editor. *The New International Dictionary of New Testament Theology, Volumes 1-3.* Grand Rapids, Michigan: Zondervan. 1981.

TDNT is an acronym for "Theological Dictionary of the New Testament." The full citation of the text is as follows: *Theological Dictionary of the New Testament.* Volumes 1-10. ed. by Gerhard Kittel. Translated by Geoffrey W. Bromiley. Grand Rapids, Michigan: Eerdmans. 1978.

TWOT is an acronym for "Theological Wordbook of the Old Testament." The full citation of the text is as follows: Theological Wordbook of the Old Testament. Volumes 1 and 2. ed. by R. Laird Harris. Chicago: Moody Press, 1980.

LXX is the acronym for the "Septuagint" named for the alleged 72 scholars who translated the Hebrew Old Testament into common Greek (about 200 B.C.E.).

MT is the acronym for the "Masoretic" text developed during the early middle ages and used as the text for the Old Testament by most Jews and Christians.

CD, or Damascus Document, was first found in a Cairo synagogue in the late nineteenth century. Later fragments of the document were found in the caves of Wâdi Qumran.

MMT, also known as 4QMMT, is an expression used in the Halakhic letter of the Dead Sea Scrolls and stands for the Hebrew *miqsat maʿaseh ha tôrā* translated "some of the deeds of Torah," a phrase found toward the end of the document (4Q399).

All sectarian documents from Qumran are labeled by the number of the cave in which the document was found, followed by "Q" for Qumran and then the fragment number (e.g., 4Q398).

The terms B.C.E. (before Common Era) and C.E. (Common Era) are alternate scholarly terms for B.C. (before Christ) and A.D. (*anno domini* "in the year of our Lord") respectively.

All scripture references in English are from the New International Version of the Bible unless otherwise indicated.

Table One: Hebrew/Aramaic Consonants and Vowels

Script	Transliteration	Pronunciation	Script	Transliteration	Pronunciation
א	ʾ	slight glottal stop	צ	ṣ	ts as in **hats**
ב	b	b as in **Betty**	ק	q	c as in **coin**
ב	b	v as in **vase**	ר	r	r as in French *rue*
ג ג	g	g as in **God**	שׁ	š	sh as in **show**
ד	d	d as in **Dad**	שׂ	ś	s as in **see**
ד	d	dh as in **Dharma**	ת	t	t as in **tea**
ה	h	h as in **haste**	ת	t	t as in **tea** or th as in **thin**
ו	w	v as in **vase**	_	a	a as in **cat**
ז	z	z as in **zoo**	_	ā	a as in **far**
ח	ḥ	h/ ch as in **Pesach**		e	e as in **met**
ט	ṭ	t as in **Tom** (emphatic)		ē	e as in **they**
י	y	y as in **yes**		i	i as in **bid**
כ ך	k	k/ ch as in **Kim** or ch as in Ger. **ich**		ō	o as in **okay**
				o	o as in **oh** (unaccented)
כ	k	ch as in Ger. **ich**		u	u as in **sue**
ל	l	l in **laugh**		ă	a as in **America**
מ	m	m as in **men**		ě	short **eh**
ם	m	m as in **men**		ŏ	short **ah**
נ	n	n as in **need**		ě	**eh** or silent
ן	n	n as in **need**	הָ	ā	a as in **ah**
ס	s	s as in **said**	׳ו	ô	o as in **open**
ע	ʿ	strong glottal stop	י	î	i as in **machine**
פ ף	p	p as in **pop** or f as in **fat**	י	ê	e as in **they**
פ	p	f as in **fat**	׳ו	û	u as in **tool**

Table Two: The Greek Alphabet

Capital Letter	Small Letter	Name	Trans-literation	Pronunciation
A	α	Alpha	a	a as in **father** (long); a as in **cat** (short)
B	β	Beta	b	b as in **bar**
Γ	γ[1]	Gamma	g	g as in **golf**
Δ	δ	Delta	d	d as in **dog**
E	ε	Epsilon	e	e as in **set**
Z	ζ	Zeta	z	z (initial) as in **zoo**; ds as in **ads**
H	η	Eta	ē	e as in **obey**
Θ	θ	Theta	th	th as in **the**
I	ι	Iota	i	i as in **magazine** (long); i as in **pill** (short)
K	κ	Kappa	k	k as in **kitten**
Λ	λ	Lambda	l	l as in **long**
M	μ	Mu	m	m as in **man**
N	ν	Nu	n	n as in **no**
Ξ	ξ	Xi	x	x as in **rex**
O	o	Omicron	o	o as in **otter**
Π	π	Pi	p	p as in **pay**
P	ρ	Rho	r	r as in **rest**
Σ	σ ς[2]	Sigma	s	s as in **sin**
T	τ	Tau	y	t as in **table**
Y	υ	Upsilon	u	u as in **user**
Φ	φ	Phi	ph	ph as in **phone**
X	χ	Chi	ch	ch as in **Christ**
Ψ	ψ	Psi	ps	ps (initial) as in **psalms**; (medial or final) as in **taps**
Ω	ω	Omega	ō	o as in **cone**

[1] When used before γ, κ, or ξ the γ is pronounced similar to ν.

[2] Form σ when beginning a word or in the middle of a word. Form ς at the end of a word (λόγος and ἐκκλησία). The pronunciation is the same for both forms.

INTRODUCTION: Why are the Dead Sea Scrolls Important to New Testament Studies?

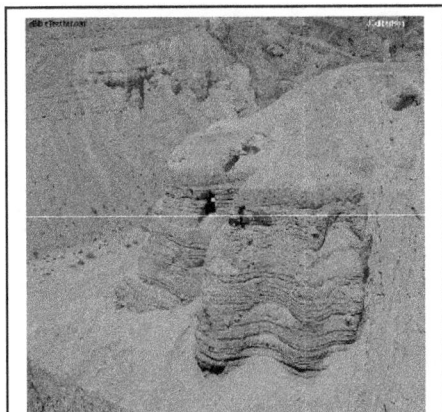

Cave Four entrance at Qumran.

A little over sixty years ago, a young Bedouin shepherd threw a stone into a hillside cave near Wâdi Qumran and heard, so the story goes, the unmistakable sound of pottery shattering. Upon checking out the source of the noise, he stumbled on what is probably the find of the century: fragments of scrolls that were obviously very old. By 1956, ten more caves were discovered, yielding archeological treasures unimagined just a few years before.

Why are these scrolls and fragments so important? The literature found in those hillside caves is significant for several reasons. First, they tell the story of an unknown group—probably Essenes[1]--who lived in the region during one of the most pivotal points in the history of western civilization: the first centuries B.C.E. and C.E.[2] From their writings we get insights into the formation of modern Judaism and primitive Christianity. Second, every book of the Old Testament was represented in those caves except the Book of Esther. By putting the fragments together and translating what remains, we have witnesses to the text of the Old Testament that are about 1000 years earlier than any previous existing witness. This is a boon to the study of the development of our Bible. Finally, the biblical texts available from the find confirm the LXX (the Greek version of the Old Testament often quoted by the New Testament writers) as a fairly accurate translation (not a paraphrase) from a Hebrew text that was available at the time of Jesus (in contrast to the Masoretic text deemed official by the Rabbis following the Jewish War of 66-70 C.E.).

The Dead Sea Scrolls have revolutionized New Testament studies. Some scholars in the past have doubted the authenticity of expressions attributed to Jesus. Scholars who approach the gospels from a form-critical point-of-view might suggest that statements attributed to Jesus had actually passed through several stages and had literary sources other than eyewitnesses.[3] These sources would stamp their own bias and predilection until the final written form bears little resemblance to the original expression.

However, some expressions found in the New Testament that once puzzled scholars can now be understood as contemporary with Jesus and His ministry because of the discovery of the scrolls. For example, we can now confirm that the utterance of Jesus on the cross, a quote of Psalm 22:1, *"Eli, Eli lema sabachthani?"* a puzzling mixture of Aramaic and Hebrew, would have been an authentic utterance of Jesus, and would not necessarily be something put in Jesus' mouth by churchmen at a later date. Like "hosanna" discussed in Chapter One, some popular expressions during the Second Temple period did not follow the standard Aramaic, as might have been expected if they were authentic to Jesus.

We also understand that "works of the Law" or more precisely "works of *tôrā*" found in Romans and Galatians, was an expression also used by the Qumran community near where the Dead Sea Scrolls were found. This was an expression that, by implication, was familiar to Jews at the time of the apostles. This provides external evidence for the dating of the letters of Paul well before the end of the first century. This phrase also helps students of the New Testament understand the context of Paul's use of the phrase in combating the influence of the "judaizers" mentioned in Galatians. It also helps imply a connection between Paul and the writers of the Dead Sea Scrolls.

Finally, students of the New Testament can better understand the messianic fervor of the period because of the Dead Sea Scrolls. We now can understand why the author of Hebrews discusses Melchizedek ("Righteous King" in Hebrew) as a type of Christ. In fact, we can infer from the Qumran documents that there was an expectation of a priestly Messiah in addition to a kingly Messiah, and that the term "Son of God" would not have been an unusual messianic title during the Second Temple period. As do the writers of the New Testament in the person of Jesus of Nazareth, the writers of the Dead Sea Scrolls bring together this mysterious connection between the eternal Melchizedek, Son of God, and messianic apocalypticism.

Who were the writers of the Dead Sea Scrolls?

The New Testament speaks of two groups of Jews that stood in opposition to Jesus: the Pharisees and the Sadducees. The Pharisees were linked with Jewish experts on the Law who were pummeled by Jesus for their adherence to oral traditions that they felt helped them keep the Law of Moses. Jesus claimed they did just the opposite (Mark 7:4-9). The Sadducees were a priestly class that owed their existence to the Temple and denied the doctrine of the resurrection (Matthew 22:23) which was held by the Pharisees, Jesus and many of the common people. In addition, Josephus describes a third group he called Essenes, who formed communities near the Dead Sea and in cities throughout Palestine.[4] Most scholars believe that the community of Qumran was Essene and that these were the people who wrote the Dead Sea Scrolls. The description of themselves in the scrolls appears similar to Josephus' description of the Essenes.

As a wrinkle in the majority view, and for reasons that should become evident in this text, the people of Qumran could very well be a sect within the sect of the Essenes. It also may be that many of these people were later influenced enough by the teachings of Christ to join the church in Jerusalem. Perhaps they encountered Jesus at His baptism. John the Baptist, himself, may have once been a member of the community.[5] Later, those from the community who had become part of the church in Jerusalem also became the backbone of the opposition to Paul's mission to the Gentiles. They became the "judaizers" who would trouble the churches that Paul helped start by insisting that converted Gentiles become Jews first (which entailed circumcision) before they could become Christians. The fight over the doctrine of justification by faith alone did not begin with Luther before the emperor at Worms in 1521, but with Paul against the judaizers from Qumran.

Author's Perspective

I come to this project with the understanding that the New Testament documents were first century documents written by eyewitnesses of the events described, by contemporaries of eyewitnesses or, in some cases, one generation removed. Though many scholars may debate the existence of a *"quelle"* or source for the synoptic gospels or speak of the New Testament in terms of layers of tradition, and though I do believe the New

Testament documents, especially the gospels, may have been edited, I do not feel that there was enough time, from the conception of the events described to the writing down of these events, for much tradition to accumulate. There just is not enough space, and this is not the chief concern in this work, to discuss effectively the arguments for or against a particular conclusion concerning the formation and dating of these documents. I leave that to better scholars than I to tackle.[6]

CHAPTER ONE: Semitisms in the New Testament and Their Relationship to the Dead Sea Scrolls

The earliest copies of the New Testament are in Greek. However, there has been speculation that some parts such as Matthew, for example, may have originally been composed in Hebrew or Aramaic.[7] Greek constructions that suggest we might be dealing with a translation of at least small portions of the New Testament from Hebrew or Aramaic are termed "Semitisms." We know that Jesus' original language was Aramaic and therefore the words of Jesus cannot be other than a translation of that language in the Greek New Testament.

The Sermon on the Mount

There are several expressions used by Jesus in the famous Sermon on the Mount (Matthew 5-7; Luke 6:17-49) that have direct and indirect parallels to expressions used by the Qumran community. For example, Jesus' reference to "poor in Spirit" is reminiscent of the language used by writers of the Qumran documents who designated themselves as "the Poor" (*ebyônîm*). Though Jesus was emphasizing spiritual poverty as warranting a blessing, not simply physical poverty, the term "poor" does have a strong economic dimension.[8] In CD 4:20-21, the commandment to do righteousness is followed by a reference to the "meek" and "poor." To be "poor" can simply mean being in an inferior social status as well as being in abject poverty. Apparently, the Qumran community felt they were both. Jesus' use of this word suggests that He knew of this community and was attempting to reply to some of their populist theology. We also can conclude that Jesus' reiteration of the Law of Moses throughout his teaching laid the groundwork for Paul's fiery opposition to using "works of *tôrā*"[9] (Chapter Two) as a way to righteousness.

The term "meek" (*ʿānāwîm*)[10] was a designation used by the Qumran community for themselves. Jesus' use of the term in Matthew 5:5 may, again, be reminiscent of language used among the Qumran community. The *ʿānāwîm* are mentioned in the Isaiah *pēšer* (4Q163, 165), the Messianic Apocalypse (4Q521, a wisdom text mentioning resurrection), Hymn of the Poor (4Q434) and the hymns from Cave One (1QHa 13:21 and 23:14), to name only a few.

Jesus would often repeat the refrain, "You have heard that it was said, but I tell you..."[11] which is remarkably similar to the refrain in MMT "Concerning [what is written]... we say." For example, 4Q396 f.1 c.2 says "...and also concerning flowing liquids, we say that in these there is no purity."[12] As a comment on *tôrā* the writer is saying here that there can be no purity of flowing liquid if the container that carries the flowing liquid is unclean. The attempt in this passage and others like it is to express the full meaning of the particular statute of *tôrā*, i.e., that there is more to a statute of *tôrā* than its surface meaning. This is precisely what Jesus is doing in the Sermon on the Mount when he uses similar language.

Jesus begins his reiteration of *tôrā* in Matthew 5:17 by quenching any rumors that he was out to do away with *tôrā* and Prophets (this can also be seen as recognition of a canon of scripture that includes at least Moses and the Prophets) but to "fulfill" it. The word "fulfill" (*plēroō*) as it relates to Scripture can have a variety of meanings including "make to come true, bring to completion, complete, accomplish, finish, and to make fully known." It would be better to understand the meaning here as "to make fully known" rather than as a prophetic "make to come true" because of the context. Jesus then tells His audience that each individual's righteousness must exceed the righteousness of the Pharisees and teachers of *tôrā* in order to enter the kingdom of heaven. "Righteousness" is, of course, a major theme in MMT, but in that document obedience to *tôrā* leads to righteousness, the assumption being that it is a real possibility for a literal obedience of *tôrā*.

Finally, in the Matthew passage, Jesus uses "you have heard that it was said, but I tell you..." to exhort, do mercy, and love one's enemies, to make clear the meaning of prohibitions against murder, adultery, divorce, and oaths in *tôrā*. Using the familiar halakhic pattern of Old Testament interpretation, Jesus warns that obedience within the verbal limitations of *tôrā* is insufficient. Though one obeys the letter of *tôrā*, he or she is still guilty of breaking *tôrā*. If one is angry as exemplified in this passage, he or she is a murderer because his contempt has rendered the object of contempt as subhuman or less valuable and, consequently, unworthy to be treated with respect as a human being in the image of God. Indeed, the Aramaic terms "*Raca*" (from *rîq* literally "empty" but here a reference to an "empty head")[13] and "*Mōre*" (from *môrôm* or "rebels" from the incident in Numbers 20:10 when Moses struck the rock in anger after the Lord had told him to speak to the rock) illustrate the teaching. The idea that this kind of anger can lead to murder is graphically illustrated in the Nazi perpetration of genocide against the Jews in the last century. Subsequently, if one has lust in the heart, he or she is already an adulterer because lust causes the one who lusts to dehumanize the object of that lust. The object is already a tool for selfish gratification whether or not one carries out the action. In addition, Jesus is saying that limiting obedience to the letter of *tôrā* rather than experiencing a change of heart could contribute to sins of omission through failure to show mercy and love as demanded by the Covenant (see Chapter Ten).

Jesus appears to be familiar with MMT. Unlike the Qumran community, however, which actually believed that it was possible to obey *tôrā*, and saw itself as a community calling Israel back to obedience to the letter of the Law, Jesus sees *tôrā* as something that is to be obeyed in the heart, not just outwardly. In fact, Jesus takes to task those who publicly appear to be the most righteous (the Pharisees) claiming that one is not righteous unless one's righteousness goes beyond that which is on public display. To the disciples of Jesus, this was an impossibility (Matthew 19:25). Paul picks up on this theme in Romans Three where he discusses a different kind of righteousness than that which comes from obedience to the Law. According to Paul, no one can obtain righteousness by obeying the Law. Instead one must obtain righteousness directly from God through Jesus.

James, who in some circles is pitted against Paul, also picks up on this theme in James 2:8-13 where he tells us if one stumbles at obeying *tôrā* at one point, that one has become a law breaker. Instead, we are under a new law—one that gives freedom (cf. Matthew 22:37-40). What is this "law that gives freedom"? James clarifies in 4:6, 7 where he tells us to submit to God and God will give grace. Though he uses different language, his message is really not unlike Paul's.[14]

"Hosanna"

"Hosanna" (*hōsanna*) is a Greek transliteration of the Hebrew word *hôšaᶜenā'* and can be found in six places in the New Testament, all in the Palm Sunday narrative of Jesus' entry into Jerusalem to mark the beginning of His Passion week. The references include three in Matthew 21 (21:9, 15), two in Mark 11:9, 10 and one in John's gospel (John 12:13). *Hôšaᶜenā'* literally means "save now" and only became settled as a liturgical element in both the Feast of Tabernacles and Passover in post-biblical Judaism. The term occurs repeatedly in the Psalms. Psalm 118:25, being part of the Hallel (Psalms 113-118) was recited in relationship to the Passover. The chant of "hosanna" on the part of the crowd as Jesus entered Jerusalem may have been a recitation of this verse.

The cry of hosanna was often accompanied by the shaking of festal branches. At the Feast of Tabernacles, the "hosanna cry" became more a shout of triumph and joy rather than a request for salvation. Psalm 118 was sometimes interpreted messianically in the Midrash and, therefore, this messianic hope would be echoed in the cry of *hôša^{ce}nā'*.[15]

A post-biblical expression of *hôša^{ce}nā'* has appeared in 4Q243 16:2 also known as Pseudo-Daniel[a]. It reads "with his great hand he will save them" and the root *yš^c* [16] follows the Hebrew form and not the expected Aramaic root *yt^c* in the otherwise Aramaic document.[17] According to Joseph Fitzmyer, this instance, along with an instance of the *yš^c* stem in an inscription found at *Tell Fakhariyah*, supports the interpretation of the form *hōsanna* as a transcription of the popular Aramaic *hôš^c n'* in the New Testament.[18]

"Overseer/Bishop"

The Hebrew word for "Overseer" (*měbaqqēr*) also translated as "Bishop,"[19] can be found in CD (4Q266 f11:16, 4Q265, 267, 269, 270, and 271) as well as in the Manuel of Discipline (4QS), and one document in Cave Five (5Q13). It appears to be behind the Greek word *episkopos* used in the New Testament (i.e., Philippians 1:1, 1 Timothy 3:1-7, Titus 1:7). *Episkopos* describes an office-holder within the church that seems parallel to that of the *měbaqqēr* in the Qumran community.[20] According to Eisenman and Wise, this "Bishop" at Qumran functions as a treasurer above the Community Council as described in the Manual of Discipline and has absolute authority over the "community and camps" in CD. According to CD 14:10, the *měbaqqēr* is the master of everyman's secrets and "tongues."[21]

The passage goes on to state that as each member enters the assembly he/she is to inform the *měbaqqēr* of any part in disputes and judgment—an activity that has some parallels with the later sacrament of confession (cf. James 5:16, 1 John 1:9). The men of the assembly are also required to provide contributions to the *měbaqqēr* and the "judges" (*šôptîm*)[22] for

16

distribution to orphans and the poor. In fact, in CD there is a note that "no one should make a deed of purchase or sale without informing the Inspector (Bishop) of the camp and making a contract (CD 13:15-16)."[23] This may be informative in helping us to understand the dealings between Peter as Bishop on the one hand, and Ananias and Sapphira on the other hand in Acts 5. This similarity of function between the *mĕbaqqēr* and the Jerusalem pastor-bishop may be direct if we understand the possibility that many of the Jerusalem church's faithful came from the Qumran community.

"The Righteousness of God"

The phrases *ṣidqat ēl* (1QS 10:25, 11:12, and 4Q256—a fragment of 1QS) and *ṣedeq ēl* (1QM 4:6 also known as "the War Scroll") share the same common stem *ṣdq* and can be translated "righteousness of God" or "justice of God." Since there is no verbatim example of this phrase in the Old Testament, the common understanding is that Paul could not have picked it up while in Israel, but must have picked it up while on one of his missionary journeys. However, after discovery of this phrase in some of the Dead Sea Scrolls, it is fairly certain that this was a well-used slogan or euphemism common in first century Palestine.[24] The phrase *ṣidqat ēl* is used in the Manuel of Discipline (1QS) in the context of the priests reciting the mighty deeds of God and His merciful favor toward Israel. The phrase *ṣedeq ēl* is used on a banner while going to war against God's enemies. Presumably, the "justice of God" is the destruction of these enemies. Paul, on the other hand, uses the phrase in Romans 3:21 to describe a righteousness that does not come from, but is known by the Law and the Prophets. It is a righteousness that comes from God and is made available to all, Jews and Gentiles alike, who trust in God on the basis of the judgment of sin in Christ Jesus.

"The Church of God"

Generally, the LXX translates *qāhāl* as *ekklesia* (Deuteronomy 4:10; 2 Chronicles 6:3), but sometimes it translates as *sunagōgē* (Jeremiah 26:17). In the New Testament, *ekklesia* became the favored expression for "church" while *sunagōgē* was reserved to speak of Jewish congregations. Paul uses the word *ekklesia* in his early letters to describe the regular, local meeting of all believers in a given location, not local home groups. In

Paul's later letters, *ekklesia* takes on eschatological significance as a heavenly reality.[25]

One of the side benefits of finding this vast store of literature at Qumran that dates to the Second Temple period is in how it can help lend support to particular variants in New Testament textual criticism. For example, in Acts 20:28 there are several variants of the phrase translated "church of God" by the United Bible Society, including "church of the Lord." According to Metzger, the external evidence supporting "church of God" and "church of the Lord" is equally balanced.[26] What might push in favor of the "harder" reading-- church of God--might be an understanding that "church of God" has an underlying Hebrew equivalent used in the community at Qumran. The Hebrew equivalent, *qāhāl ēl* can be found in a number of Qumran documents including 4QM 4:10 and 4Q377 f2 c2:6.

"the Many"

The phrase "the Many" is used in the Manual of Discipline and in other Qumran texts such as the Damascus Document. In CD (4Q266 f11:1) "the Many" refers to the congregation of the faithful, but is literally translated as "the Many" directly from the Hebrew.[27]   The Hebrew word for "the Many" appears to be underlying the Greek *tōn pleionōn*, which literally means "the Many" or "the Majority," and is used by several New Testament writers including Paul in such passages as Matthew 26:28, Mark 14:24, Luke 22:20, Acts 6:2 5, 15:12, 30; and 2 Corinthians 2:5-6. Subsequently, the Qumran texts help us understand that the New Testament writers are also probably referring to the congregation of the faithful, perhaps a local church or smaller gathering of the faithful as in the case of Paul.

"Circumcision of the Heart"

This phrase can be found negatively in Jeremiah 9:26, Ezekiel 44:7 and 9. In Deuteronomy 30:6, circumcision of the heart is something that God does so that we might love Him with all our heart and soul fulfilling the terms of Deuteronomy 6:5. The Habukkuk *pēšer* (1QpHab 11:13) has the phrase *mûl 'at ʿārlat leb* "circumcise the foreskin of the heart."   The context of the *pēšer* involves an interpretation of Habukkuk 2:16 in which God judges the priest for public drunkenness. His shame exceeds his glory because of his failure to "circumcise the foreskin of his heart."

In Romans 2:29, Paul speaks of *tomē kardias* "circumcision of the heart" as a work of the Spirit in contrast to "the written code" which does nothing to change the heart. This is in stark contrast to the Qumran documents which describe *tomē kardias* as something coupled to the circumcision of the flesh and obedience to *tôrā*. Paul severs *tomē kardias* from circumcision of the flesh and even contrasts the two. Then he ties *tomē kardias* with a direct work of the Spirit. Only as the heart is changed, says Paul, can one truly obey the spirit and intention of *tôrā*. Paul writes in the spirit of Deuteronomy 30:6 but carefully strikes a contrast between himself and the Qumran community. He believes righteousness comes by grace through faith, but they believe righteousness comes by strict obedience to *tôrā* (see Chapter Two).

"Sons of Light"

This phrase (*huioi phōtos*) is used by John (John 12:36), and by Paul (1 Thessalonians 5:5), and also quite extensively by the sectarians at Qumran. John writes of Jesus telling his listeners that they are sons of light when they put their trust in Him. Paul uses the phrase to differentiate from those in darkness; who are drunk and not alert and prepared for "the day of the Lord." In 4Q174 (4QFlorilegium) the "sons of light" (*bênî ʾôr*) are contrasted with the "sons of Belial" (*bênî bliyyaʿal*) who come against the "sons of light" with the "plans of Belial" (*běmaḥšěbôt bliyyaʿal*).[28]

"Belial/Beliar"

Before the finding of the Dead Sea Scrolls, scholars were curious as to why Paul would use this apparent name for the devil[29] in 2 Corinthians 6:15, the only place in the New Testament where the word *beliar* can be found. In the Old Testament, the word (*bliyyaʿal*)[30] can be found in several places. In Deuteronomy 13:14 it is used to describe "wicked men" who lead a town away from the Lord to worship idols. The context informs us that if a town allows this to occur, all its inhabitants should be put to the sword; they should receive the ban (*ḥāram*).[31] This ban was applied to certain "wicked men" in Judges 19:22 and 20:13 who had demanded that an old man of Gibeah, of Benjamin, hand over one of his overnight guests, a Levite, so they could "have sex with him."[32] Instead, they were given a concubine whom they raped and killed, thus provoking the ban.

Hannah did not want to be perceived as a drunken or "wicked woman" in 1 Samuel 1:16 Eli's sons were seen as "wicked men" in 1 Samuel 2:12 because "they had no regard for the Lord," and in 1 Samuel 10:27 the word is applied to certain "troublemakers" who insulted Saul after he was made king over Israel. In 1 Kings 21:10 and 13 the word is applied to "scoundrels" who unjustly denounced Naboth to Ahab causing his death. Some "scoundrels" also opposed Rehoboam, son of Solomon, when he was young in 2 Chronicles 13:7. Proverbs 19:28 speaks of "a rascal" making a mockery of justice when he bears witness. In Psalm 41:8, a disease can be considered *bliyya^{c}al* when it leads to death. Accordingly, counsel against the Lord (Nahum 1:11) is also *bliyya^{c}al*. In fact, anything that offends the justice of God is considered *bliyya^{c}al* (Psalms 101:3) including harboring "wicked thoughts" (Deuteronomy 15:9). "Evil men" are fodder for the fire (2 Samuel 23:6; cf. Proverbs 6:12). In Job 34:18, God is differentiated from "wicked" men because He does not pervert justice as they do. They are considered "destroyers" in Nahum 2:2. Finally, *bliyya^{c}al* is "destruction" in the context of 2 Samuel 22:5 and Psalm 18:4.

In the Qumran documents, *bliyya^{c}al* is mentioned in several contexts, but is not found in other literature of its time, which might lead one to think that it was a popular designation only to those at Qumran and those, like Paul, who might have had to deal with their doctrines.[33] As mentioned above, 4Q174 discusses "sons of Belial" coming against the "sons of light" with the "plans"[34] of Belial. 4Q286 f.7 c.2 is a ritualized condemnation of the devil, (or one who is wicked) or possibly an excommunication ritual.[35] In this text, Belial is plotting some hostile activity, is intercepted and then condemned along with the "sons of Belial." A general condemnation is offered against all who plan wicked activity, and plot to "alter"[36] the precepts of *tôrā*. Jesus may be responding to a charge of "altering" precepts of *tôrā* in Matthew 5:17.[37]

"Messenger of Satan"

In 4Q390 f. 2, *bliyya^{c}al* is mentioned in conjunction with "rule" (*memšālā*).[38] This "rule of Belial" is the same as being put under the rule of the angels (messengers) of Mastemoth. Who are these angels of Mastemoth? The phrase means "angels of destruction."[39] The only reference in Scripture to "mastemoth" is in Hosea 9:7-8 where *mastēmā* is translated "hostility" in the New American Standard translation. The reference in Hosea 9 and the context of 4Q390 f 2 and 4Q387 f 2 (4QPseudo-Moses b) suggest that these angels are fallen angels unleashed by God as a form of punishment for sin. This language is strikingly similar to the language of Paul when he says I have "given [someone] over to Satan for the destruction of his flesh (1 Corinthians 5:4-5)," a procedure used against someone who claims to be a member of the community but refuses to repent—resulting in excommunication. In fact, *mastēmā* and *sātān* share a similar consonant cluster *stm/n*.[40] Finally, if we have correctly understood the etymological relationship between *mastēmā* and *sātān*, the phrase "messengers of Satan" (*angelos satana*) in 2 Corinthians 12:7 is a Semitism and may have been a popular euphemism in the Second Temple period.

CHAPTER TWO: "Works of Torah" in Paul and Qumran

The phrase *ma^{c}ăśeh ha tôrā*[41] is found in fragment two of 4Q398 and in 4Q399. These fragments, in turn, appear to be only part of a larger halakhot (ruling on Jewish law) addressed to those who were faithful to Qumran teaching. The translation of this phrase into Greek (*ergōn nomou*) is only found in Paul's response to the "judaizers" in Galatians and Romans and is not found in other literature of the time or in rabbinic literature. This suggests that Paul was writing in response to Jewish believers in Jesus who were also sympathizers with the Qumran philosophy, and not in response to rabbinic interpretations of the Law as represented by the Pharisees.[42]

Even the rabbis from the pharisaic tradition did not believe that *tôrā* could be applied literally. They had engineered a "hedge (of oral tradition) around *tôrā*" which later came to be known as the Mishnah. The rabbis believed the oral tradition came from God just as *tôrā*, but the New Testament writers claimed this oral tradition *de facto* replaced the Law. The Qumran sect, however, actually believed righteousness could be gained by strictly adhering to the letter of the Law. Those from the Qumran sect probably believed the Pharisees were heretics (e.g. not strict enough)!

In 4Q398 f. 1 there is a discussion of blessing and cursing "written in the book of Moses," referring to Deuteronomy 27-28, and an exhortation to "remember the kings of Israel and reflect on their deeds, how whoever of them respected [the Torah] was freed from his afflictions."[43] Apparently in a continuation of this discussion in 4Q399, fragment one exhorts the reader to "remember David, one of the Pious (*ḥāssîdîm*)" who was "freed from his many afflictions and was forgiven." The title of "Pious," actually a variation of the word *ḥesed* or "unfailing love (see Chapter Ten)," is a reference to the "men of piety" (*ănšē ḥesed*) in passages like Isaiah 57:1, those who are faithful to God's covenant (with Moses, giver of the Law). David is best remembered by keeping "works of *tôrā*" which the Qumran writer says "we think (or reckon)[44] are good for you."

In the second column of that same fragment, the reader is exhorted in context to reflect on *tôrā*, which presumably means do "works of *tôrā*." Upon doing so, the reader would be reckoned righteous (*wnḥšbh lk lṣdqh* or "and be regarded as righteous").[45]   Most scholars agree that when the Qumran text writers spoke of this "reckoning" they were referring to Psalm 106:31 which speaks of Phineas the high priest standing up against "sacrifices to lifeless gods" offered by pagans. Paul, on the other hand, uses the text in Genesis 15:6 which attributes righteousness to Abraham because he believed God. To the Qumran devotees, "reckoning" as righteous means obedience to *tôrā*. In CD (4Q266), the one reckoned is among the sons of truth and is not among those who have rejected the "Foundations of Righteousness" or *tôrā*. In 4Q458, the Lord "justifies" (*sdq* "it makes righteous") one, and that one "walks on high."[46]   It is unclear from *this* text how the Lord justifies, but it would appear that the result is that one walks with God.

Here is the point of contention between Paul and the Qumran community. Paul attributes the faith of Abraham as warranting a reckoning to righteousness (Galatians 3:6-9). In fact, in the context of Galatians 3, Paul goes on to state that anyone who seeks to become righteous by "works of *tôrā*" is under a curse, because, in Paul's theology, failure to keep the entire Law perfectly brings the curse (Galatians 3:10, a reference to Deuteronomy 27:26). It is interesting how Paul deals with the apparent pervasiveness of this Qumran philosophy of "works-righteousness" among Jewish believers. For as we have seen, these references to cursing and blessing were in the same context as the Qumran sectarian discussion of faithfulness to do "works of *tôrā*" as a means of achieving righteousness. However, the text of Deuteronomy 27 deals with specific actions that violate the Ten Commandments. Paul brings up these actions in Romans 2:17-24 and throws them in the face of Qumran sympathizers. The Gentiles blaspheme God because these people demonstrate that an attempt at becoming righteousness through strict obedience to *tôrā* doesn't work (Isaiah 52:5; Ezekiel 36:22).

By comparing the Qumran literature to the book of Acts, we discover more evidence that the main source of the judaizing pressure on the Jerusalem church came from Qumran sympathizers. For example, in Acts 6:7 Luke remarks that "a great crowd (*polus ochlos*) of priests became obedient to the faith." This, on the surface, appears contradictory to Acts 4:1 which shows the "priests" to be hostile to the new faith. According to Longenecker and Jeremias, there were as many as eight thousand ordinary priests and ten thousand Levites serving in the temple whose social position was decidedly inferior to that of the high priestly families in

23

Jerusalem.[47] Luke may knowingly or unknowingly be referring to priests from the high priestly families in 4:1 and socially inferior priests in 6:7. It is from these socially inferior priests that the Qumran population was largely drawn. The documents from the Qumran community also testify to claims that many of the people from that community were of Zadokite or priestly descent.

The judaizers may very well have originated from Qumran, were converted to faith in Yeshua, and brought their teaching concerning "works of *tôrā*" with them. They looked to James, brother of Jesus, as their champion. However, according to Longenecker, James, speaking before the Council in Jerusalem in Acts 15, shifted the discussion of conversion of the Gentiles from a proselyte model to an eschatological model.[48] What this means is that James left no doubt that the outcome would be favorable to Paul. His speech bypassed any insistence that Gentiles convert to Judaism to become Christians and proposed instead that Jewish believers listen to Amos (Amos 9:10-11) who spoke of God taking a people for Himself among the Gentiles. To gentile believers, he only asked that they consider Jewish sensitivities by refusing any hint of sexual immorality, and the eating of blood and animals offered to idols (see Chapter Three).

It is very interesting that James used a quotation from Amos that was closer to the LXX than to the Masoretic text. The LXX preserves a variant from the Masoretic text that lends itself better to the interpretation of Amos that James gives. Some have argued that this proves that Luke or a later redactor was putting these words in James' mouth because a non-Hellenized Jew in Jerusalem would not quote the LXX.[49] However, there is another option. At Qumran in Cave Four, a document was found quoting Amos 9 in Hebrew using a text identical to the one used in Acts.[50] This would suggest that there may be a Hebrew variant upon which this text from the LXX was based and that this variant was in circulation at the time of Jesus.[51] James was using a Hebrew text that was in use by the Essene community at Qumran to speak directly to those judaizers from that community who had come into the church with their demand that all believers do "works of *tôrā*."

Some, such as Eisenman and Wise, see James as a champion of the judaizers and will cite James' teaching on works-righteousness in James 2:14f as evidence of real opposition to Paul. It is probably true that the

24

judaizers saw James as a champion of their cause before the Council in Jerusalem in 49 C.E.[52] Indeed, James appears to contradict Paul in James 2:24 when he says "that a person is justified by what he does and not by faith alone (NIV)." This seems very similar to the language of the halakhic letter mentioned above:

> "And it shall be reckoned to you as righteousness[53] when you do what is upright and good before him…(4Q399, fragment 1, column 2:4)"

However, James is not contradicting Paul and supporting the Qumran teaching even in this epistle. Note that James never attributes a reckoning of righteousness to works of *tôrā* as does MMT. In fact, whereas the Qumran teachers might look to Psalm 106:31 as their "reckoning" model; James, like Paul, looks to Abraham who *believed* God and was reckoned righteous. James is simply clarifying what it means to believe. True faith is faith that is accompanied by works (not necessarily works of *tôrā*) or things that we do that demonstrate that we actually believe. We are never saved by a "faith" that does not produce fruit, to use Paul's language (Galatians 5:16-26). This is made clear by James' use of the story of Rahab the prostitute. She could have said she believed the testimony of the Israelites about their God, but she would have denied this belief if she had not hid the spies.

I believe that the conciliation of James with Paul effectively put an end to the judaizer influence and marked the beginning of the end for the church in Jerusalem. Events of the next two decades would see a rise of Jewish nationalism that would eventually break out into open warfare with Rome. Any attempt by Jews to cooperate with Gentiles would bring undue hardship to that Jew in Jerusalem. We know that eventually James lost his life. However, the decision of the Council was a great victory for the gospel of Grace first preached by Jesus himself. The thinking of the judaizers became further marginalized as the church became more and more gentile. These judaizers may have merged with the heretical Ebionites,[54] whose philosophy has been revived in part in some quarters of the modern Messianic movement.[55]

CHAPTER THREE: Purification Concerns

In order to understand Paul's views and actions in regard to ceremonial purity in general and Temple purity in particular, one must first understand general attitudes in the Jewish community during the Second Temple period and second, understand the attitudes of Jesus toward purity. Both the cultural milieu and Jesus' behavior and teaching in confrontation with this culture have their effect on Paul.

Jewish Views on Purity

The New Testament in Mark 7:3-4 and Matthew 15:1-2 has an incident involving the Pharisees in dispute with the disciples of Jesus over ceremonial washing of hands and implements before eating. The Pharisees and other Jews of the time that would emulate them, followed "the tradition of the elders" (known later from writings that would become the Mishnah) which advocated ceremonial washing of the hands along with cups, pitchers and kettles used in the preparation of food. Archaeological evidence confirms Jewish concerns over purity during the Second Temple period. From excavations in Galilee, stone vessels of chalk or limestone are widely in evidence.[56]   According to the Mishnah[57] stone vessels are impervious to impurity, and because they are inexpensive, it would make sense that they would be the implement of choice in the handling of food.

In addition to the widespread use of these stone vessels, archaeologists have uncovered numerous step pools or *miqwāôt* —ritual baths, particularly concentrated in Galilee, Judea and the Golan, but noticeably lacking along the coast, in Samaria and east of the Jordan. Well placed step pools would aide the Jewish faithful in their quest to maintain ceremonial purity. This concentration of *miqwāôt* would coincide with known Jewish habitation during the Second Temple period.

miqwāôt at Qumran

The Qumran community held purity concerns to be of the utmost importance. Special vessels for the handling of food and *miqwā̊ôt* can be found among the ruins of the community. In fact, the community may have used *miqwā̊ôt* exclusively. Though probably written before the time of Jesus, there is an interesting criticism in 4Q262 of Jews who would baptize in the flowing rivers such as the Jordan River. For the people of this community, no one can get atonement by his acts through sea or river purification.

Though reflective of a somewhat narrow sectarian viewpoint, this community had a much greater influence on Jews of this period (cf. Chapter Two) than might otherwise be expected. 1QSa 2:3-10 provides purity rules governing attendance at the "assembly" (*qāhāl*) under the authority of priests. First, no man defiled (*nāgaᶜ*)[58] by "the impurities of man" can enter the assembly. The phrase "impurities of man" was apparently a euphemism for emission of semen[59] and is found elsewhere in 4Q249. 4Q274 f1c1 delineates an interpretation of Leviticus 15 that governs emissions of semen[60] and menstrual bleeding.

Men and women who have such emissions are considered unclean and anyone who touches such persons is considered unclean for seven days, shall not eat, and must bathe after contact. He or she is treated as though they have touched a corpse. Second, anyone defiled in the flesh (e.g., paralysis in the feet, blemishes visible to the eye, tottering in the elderly) cannot enter the congregation (1QSa c2 7). At Qumran, the purity regulations of Leviticus 11-15 are dissected and applied to almost every possible scenario, continually governing every area of social life within the community.

Jesus and Purity

The understanding that impurity and sin in *tôrā* are not the same is the backdrop for Jesus' teaching on purity. In other words, to be in a state of impurity because of some bodily function or disease is not in itself wrong.[61] However, to deliberately breach purity regulations is sin (Leviticus 19:8, 20:17 and 22:9).

Ceremonial Hand Washing. Both Matthew 15:3-20 and Mark 7:6-23 are parallel accounts of Jesus' confrontation with the Pharisees and Scribes over ceremonial hand washing. Each begins with ceremonial hand washing, and both go on to present Jesus' clarification about "uncleanness." That is, it is not as important what goes into a person's mouth as what proceeds out of it from the heart. Matthew's gospel leaves out some details that Mark's includes. For example, Mark's gospel has an introductory explanation about ceremonial washings extending to the cups, pitchers and kettles, which the Pharisees and their followers practice; whereas, Matthew's gospel does not. Mark's gospel identifies Corbin as the name for the practice of giving to the Temple money that was supposed to be set aside to assist aged parents. Matthew's gospel describes the practice, but does not give the name. Finally, when Jesus gives a halakhic pronouncement on what makes a person unclean, both Matthew and Mark provide similar details, but Mark explains that Jesus is pronouncing all foods clean (*katharizōn panta ta brōmata*). He apparently supplies the added information for the benefit of his audience: largely Gentile readers in Rome. Matthew, on the other hand, has a primarily Jewish intended audience who would recognize the significance of this discussion without a need for cultural and religious explanations.

Significantly, Jesus did two things in this exchange. First, Jesus was carefully announcing an impending change in the applicability of levitical kosher regulations as a means of gaining or keeping holiness. He was not telling his Jewish listeners that they may disregard kosher regulations. In fact, one could argue from the context that Jesus was confining his discussion to otherwise kosher or "clean" foods made unclean, according to Pharisaic practice, by failure to perform additional ceremonial washings not prescribed in *tôrā*.[62]

However, there is enough ambiguity in the story that Mark would clarify for his gentile readers that Jesus was anticipating a time when his disciples (largely gentile) would not be bound by levitical regulations, but would be bound by a new condition of the heart. This new situation will be reiterated in Acts 10 when Peter gets a vision of the sheet with the animals. When told by a voice, presumably the resurrected Christ, "Kill and eat," Peter was horrified, but Jesus would go on to say, "Do not call anything impure that God has made clean."

It is important here to note that Luke, in presenting this story, was referring to Ezekiel 4:14, a similar time of great change when the prophet Ezekiel was called upon to eat unclean food among Gentiles.[63] It was unlikely that the sheet with animals entirely violated kosher requirements:

probably, the animals were both clean and unclean. The point is that this is an apocalyptic time in which Gentiles would be coming into the Kingdom of God and the levitical laws will not apply to them. The formerly unclean Gentiles and "clean" Jews would be together as one (Galatians 3:28). That which was formerly unclean will become clean and dwell in the Kingdom of God with the already clean. This new situation is in focus in the discussion that follows this pericope—that of Jesus and the woman of Tyre. Here, even Gentile "dogs" can, by faith, participate in the Kingdom of God.

The second thing Jesus did was refocus the intent of *tôrā* declaring all intentional breaches of holiness (purity) regulations as sin. Jesus made uncleanness, and its intentional breach a matter of the heart and not merely external or ceremonial. Jesus was the "fulfillment" of these regulations whether ceremonial or moral (p. 10). He was making a statement concerning the coming of the Kingdom of God. The situation has changed. In the past, holiness was demonstrated by a certain way of life that would set his people off from others, but now holiness is demonstrated by acknowledging the presence of the King and deferring to Him. He is with them and holiness will come from within (Mark 1:15, Luke 17:21).

Woman with an Issue of Blood. Luke 8 has the story of the woman "subject to bleeding." The story tells of the woman's desperation for she had been bleeding for twelve years. When she went up to Jesus and touched him—hoping for anonymity with the crowd—she was healed. However, Jesus wanted to use the situation to address the purity regulations found in Leviticus 15. Jesus deliberately points up the fact that he was touched by this woman who, according to Leviticus 15:25 was unclean.

By most accounts, Jews of the Second Temple period (especially so those influenced by Qumran teaching) would consider Jesus to be unclean when the woman touched Him. In fact, a case could be made that the woman sinned by deliberately breaching purity regulations. Yet we have no indication that Jesus went home, washed and changed his clothes as Leviticus 15:27 says one must. Instead, Jesus uses the incident to force his audience to make a choice about Him. Either Jesus is a confirmed sinner as the Pharisees would insist, or the situation has indeed changed: the Kingdom of God has come. Jesus didn't violate *tôrā* regulations; He fulfilled them, and the woman was now healed. Jesus was not unclean as a result of her touch. The opposite was true: the woman was clean by His touch. The woman had an encounter with Christ and now was no longer unclean.

The Cleansing of the Temple. Apparently, Jesus had to cleanse the temple twice for John speaks of a cleansing of the Temple early in Jesus' ministry (John 2:12-17) when Jesus angrily denounces the making of the place of worship into a market place, while the other gospels speak of a cleansing right before the week of His passion (Matthew 21:12, 13; Mark 11:15-17; Luke 19:45-46). In the synoptic accounts, this second cleansing has the added dimension of Jesus offering an interpretation of Jeremiah 7:11. The context of the Jeremiah passage has God telling his people that they need to alter their ways and actions when they make a pretense of worship at the Temple. They are not to practice idolatry, commit adultery, steal, murder, or bear false witness. They also must not oppress orphans, the fatherless and the alien—or non-Israelite.[64] It is clear that Jesus is linking what is going on in the Temple with these practices.

Not only are they breaking the Ten Commandments, a reminder of the revelry while Moses was on Mount Sinai, but they were depriving the Gentile of the opportunity to approach God. Most likely, the outer court or court of the Gentiles—a place set aside for God-fearing Gentiles and common people to approach God (Ezekiel 42:14, 44:19, 46:20; Revelation 11:2)—was being utilized for this market place. Paul also picks up on this theme when he quotes from Isaiah 52:5 and Ezekiel 36:22 in Romans 2:24: "God's name is blasphemed among the Gentiles because of you." Jesus was making a statement at the second cleansing that though these Jews might have thought they were ceremonially clean, they were not clean before God. Also, those whom the Jews disdained—the Gentiles— were now clean because the Kingdom of God is present in the person of Christ.

Paul and Purity

Paul follows Jesus' explanation that the Kingdom of God is present. Everything has changed because of the coming of Christ. All concerns about the Old Testament purity regulations are now secondary in light of the new situation. What is important is to love God and love one's neighbor (Samaritans, Gentiles) as oneself as Jesus had admonished his followers (Matthew 22:37-40, Mark 12:29-31)

Paul takes on the question of what to do about eating meat sacrificed to idols in 1 Corinthians 10:23-33 and Romans 14:13-21. In Rome and Corinth, the best meat sold in the market place would most likely be meat offered to a pagan idol. The question arose, should Christians eat such meat? We know from Acts 21 that James had written to the Gentile churches that believers should abstain from meat offered to idols. Does Paul now contradict him here? Paul's discussion of whether or not one can eat meat offered to idols comes out of a halakhic description of Exodus 32:6. In this story, the children of Israel coming out of Egypt made an idol and offered sacrifices to it while Moses was on Mount Sinai receiving the Ten Commandments. The text goes on to describe a night of sexual revelry.[65] Paul then admonishes the Corinthians to avoid idol worship in all its forms and warns of its close association with sexual immorality. With this background, Paul tackles the question of eating meat offered to idols. Generally, he says, when one is eating at someone's home and meat is placed before him, one should not worry about whether or not the meat was offered to an idol, but instead give thanks to God. Paul cites Psalm 24:1 for support. God has changed the situation. It is not what goes into a man that makes a man unclean, but what comes from the heart.

This leads to the second part of the discussion. If someone raises the issue that the meat could have been offered to an idol, one should not eat it because the eating would damage the conscience of the one who raised the issue. One would not be acting in love, if one would go on to eat in the presence of one concerned about this issue. This is Paul's point: do not deliberately eat meat if it will harm the conscience of anyone present because to do so would be to act in an unloving manner. Love is the important thing (1 Corinthians 13:13). Paul tells the Corinthians to obey James because to do so would be unloving toward James and Jewish believers. This is true even though idols are nothing and we have liberty to eat everything.

The Temple

According to Josephus, the animosity of the Jews toward foreign gifts and sacrifice at the Temple on behalf of a gentile rose to extreme heights just before outbreak of war with Rome in 66 C.E.[66] Indeed, a blanket refusal to sacrifice on behalf of the emperor led directly to war with Rome. It is clear from documents at Qumran and allusions to this topic in Acts and Galatians that the events leading to the Jewish war with Rome were the culmination of many years of seething resentment.

When Paul arrived at Jerusalem, according to Acts 21:17-26, he was warmly greeted by a contingent from that church and was then brought to James and the elders of the church there. It is clear from the context that all, including James, praised God for Paul's work among the Gentiles.

Second Temple Reproduction
(Wikipedia)

Then, in v. 21 they report to Paul that some of the Jews in the Jerusalem church were believing rumors that Paul was telling Jews that lived among the Gentiles not to follow Jewish customs. Then they asked him to join with them in purification rites before going to the Temple to demonstrate that there was no truth to these rumors. Paul complies, not because he is under compulsion by James, but by God because of love (Romans 14:13-21). The rumor mongers of whom Paul was informed were likely from the Qumran community or others who sympathized with their aims and the reason the rumors were being spread was due to the extreme xenophobia coming from this community. Paul was marked as an associate with Gentiles, would bring gentile gifts (monies collected from the churches for the church in Jerusalem) to the Temple, and even (allegedly) bring Gentiles themselves into the inner court of the Temple.

Ezekiel 44:5-9 provides an exhortation to the prophet to confront inattention to regulations regarding the Temple. The focus here is to the entrance and exits of the Temple area. Pointedly, foreigners "uncircumcised in heart and flesh" are not allowed in God's sanctuary (*miqdāš*) or holy place. Apparently, the people of Israel were allowing Gentiles to go beyond the court of the Gentiles and into the holy place itself at this time. Also, according to the text, the people were allowing those who were not Levites or Zadokites to operate as priests, permitting them to offer fat and blood as part of their sacrifices.

The Qumran documents, obviously concerned with the same issues brought up by Ezekiel, abound with exhortations concerning Temple purification. The Temple Scroll (11Q19) provides examples in column 50 and in 11Q20 fragments 13-19. 11Q19 column 53 and elsewhere relates the importance of not eating blood. This concern was so strong in the community that James may have felt the need to put it at the top of his list in his farewell to Paul. James relayed to Paul that Gentile believers must respect Jewish sensitivities in this area along with avoiding food sacrificed to idols, meat from strangled animals, and sexual immorality (Acts 20:25

Purification pertaining to the Temple is a major theme in MMT. In 4Q394, there is a discussion of wheat grown by Gentiles and brought to the Temple as an offering. Presumably, this was wheat grown and processed by Gentiles and sold to an Israelite. Therefore, it was unclean, and no unclean wheat can be brought into the Temple.

Gentiles touching such wheat defile it, making it inedible to an Israelite. In 4Q395 the sacrifice of Gentiles is looked upon disapprovingly. In 4Q396 fragment 1, column 2 and again in 4Q397 fragments 3 and 4, there is a discussion of Temple purity with respect to flowing liquids and their containers.[67] Of particular concern is the use of animal skins which, in this context, carries gentile gifts, and are therefore prohibited in the Temple. These skins are not a part of the Temple sacrifice itself and come under *tôrā* prohibition not to touch the carcass of a dead animal (Leviticus 11:26, 37-40; see also Judges 14:8, 9).

4Q458, an apocalyptic fragment, makes mention (unfavorably) of pollution (*tûmā*) and fornication (*z^enût*), themes related to the Temple and recall the exhortation that James gave to Paul in Acts 15:29. Eisenman and Wise continually read conflict between Paul and James into the Qumran texts over notions of righteousness (see Chapter Two). According to Eisenman and Wise, 4Q458 makes mention of those who were "justified and walked according to the Laws."[68] However, this is a mistranslation. It actually reads "justified him and went on high" (*ṣdqu w^e hlk ^{c}l hrôm*)[69] In the same context, the one who justifies also "swallows" or "destroys" (*bāla^c*). The word *bāla^c* is linguistically related to "Baalam" and "Belial," the latter used at Qumran as a name for the devil. For the former, see 2 Peter 2:15 and Jude 11 where Baalam is used in conjunction with "wickedness." In the context of 4Q458, presumably the Lord or Messiah will destroy the uncircumcised (typical xenophobic expression at Qumran) and completely counter in sentiment and practice to Paul's mission to the Gentiles.

In Chapter Two, we learned that the Qumran writers probably cited Phineas' reckoning as righteous in Psalm 106:31 in their argument for "works-righteousness." This was, of course, in opposition to Paul's citation of Abraham in his argument for "faith-righteousness." The story of Phineas, grandson of Aaron, is found in Numbers 25. In the context, Phineas was zealous for the honor of God when the Israelites turned away from God to Moabite gods and sexual immorality. The link between sexual immorality and idolatry is clear at Qumran, and this link can even be found in the New Testament in the agreement between James and Paul (Acts 15:29), as we have already seen.

In the Numbers 25 account, Israel began turning toward idols and sexual immorality. This event followed the unsuccessful attempt by Balaam to curse Israel at the request of Balak, King of Moab. After the fourth oracle of Balaam's prophetic utterances, the text has both Balak and Balaam each going his own way. It seems, however, that something else must have transpired between them to suggest the animosity toward Balaam in both testaments following this account (Numbers 31:8; Deuteronomy 23:4, 5; Joshua 13:22, 24:9, 10; Nehemiah 13:2; Micah 6:5; 2 Peter 2:15, Revelation 2:14). The passage in Revelation 2:14 is particularly telling because the counsel that Balaam gave to Balak to entice the Israelites to idolatry and sexual immorality is not explicitly mentioned in the Old Testament account, but can be inferred.[70] John, in writing Revelation, may have had access to other sources not available to us. There is nothing at Qumran to corroborate this scenario. Nevertheless, the attitude and extant writings do confirm hostility toward Gentiles, their gifts, and the association of Gentiles with sexual immorality.

CHAPTER FOUR: Messianism and Melchizedek

Two of the more complete fragments, aptly named "the Messianic Apocalypse (4Q521)" and "11QMelchizedek (11Q13)" are fascinating in that both speak of a single messianic individual identified with the personage of Isaiah 61:1-2. It is important to point out that most scholars would deny that there is any real messianic reference in the Old Testament prior to the composition of Daniel.[71] In the strict sense, this is absolutely true. Virtually none of the prophets and writers of the Old Testament were apocalyptic. Rather, they attributed their *māšîăḥ* figures to people living during their time. It is only during post-biblical, but pre-Christian times that the Jewish people began to see a second, more prophetic side to what we understand today as messianic prophesies. This, in itself, is important for New Testament studies because we can know from the Qumran documents that the New Testament writers were not unique in seeing allusions to *māšîăḥ* throughout the Old Testament.

Both the Dead Sea Scrolls and the New Testament recognized many of the same Old Testament passages as messianic. In addition to Isaiah 61:1-2, we have the Melchizedek scriptures in Genesis 14:18 and Psalm 104. These passages hint at the eternal nature of this mysterious person. Both the Dead Sea Scrolls and the New Testament link them together with Messiah.

Also, we know from scattered references in the Qumran documents that the community apparently believed in an apocalyptic visitation of at least two messiahs: one royal (the Messiah of Israel) and another, more prominent priestly one (the Messiah of Aaron).[72] We are familiar with a royal Messiah descending from the line of David (see Chapter Five), but it is not entirely clear how the Qumran community got its expectation of a priestly Messiah of Aaron. Fitzmyer suggests that they may have come to this view based on Zechariah 6:12-15[73] which mentions a priest who wears a crown, builds the Temple of the Lord, works in harmony with the king, and "whose name is the Branch." It is likely that this "branch" imagery was meant to speak, as the context suggests, of one who branches out to build the temple. It is also highly likely, however, that Jews in the apocalyptic era of the first century related this passage to Jeremiah 23:5-6 and Jeremiah 33:15-16 which was seen by that time to be messianic.[74] For the early Christian community, which also understood these passages to be messianic, the duality of the messiah was seen not as a duality of persons, for the priest and king were one and the same (Romans 1:3 and Hebrews 4:14), but a duality of visitation (1 Thessalonians 4:13-17 and Revelation 19:11-16).

This dual messiah appears in passages such as 1QS 9:11 "...until the prophet comes and the Messiahs of Aaron and Israel."[75] Presumably, the prophet (*nābî*) would be Elijah the prophet who was taken to heaven (2 Kings 2:11) without having died and was popularly thought, and is thought even to this day to precede the coming of Messiah (Malachi 4:4, 5). This dual messiah seems to appear again in 1QSa 2:11-21. Although, identification of the priest mentioned in this document as the Messiah of Aaron, may be presumptuous, it does seem likely that this passage is a mention of two messiahs with the priestly Messiah (Messiah of Aaron) presiding in a superior position to the Messiah of Israel. What is remarkable about this passage is two-fold.

First, 2:11b-12a says "when God begets (*yālad*) the Messiah with them"[76] appears to be saying that God has a father-son relationship with the Messiah of Israel. Of course, this is one possible explanation in light of the "Son of God" document discussed in the next chapter. The use of "begat" could also be a figurative discussion of one "bringing forth" or initiating a special event, as in Job 38:29. However, in light of everything we know of this community, it is more likely that the writer had Psalm 2:7 in mind, where a father-son relationship and the initiation of a special event are both in view.

Second, the event is the installation of the Messiah of Israel with the community and priest (Messiah of Aaron) gathered at a community supper. The community supper may be a celebration of covenant (*brît*). Indeed, there is an association of food, or more properly, a sacrifice with covenant in the Old Testament. In Genesis 15:18 God and Abraham establish a covenant that involved the cutting in half of a heifer, goat and ram, along with a dove and young pigeon. The Passover meal involves a sacrifice and is a celebration of the covenant that God remembered in Exodus 2:24. Psalm 50:5 also speaks of a gathering together of consecrated individuals to celebrate covenant with a sacrifice. This would-be celebration of covenant presided over by the Messiah of Israel is a startling parallel to the celebration of the New Covenant by Jesus of

Nazareth who, with His twelve disciples offers up his broken body and shed blood as a sacrifice.

In CD 8:18-20, the writer speaks of new converts who, presumably, join the community and enter the "covenant." One of the goals of new converts in 1QS 8 is to eat of "the pure food of the men of holiness."[77] The community may have the "new covenant" of Jeremiah 31:31-33 in mind in which the prophet promises a future time when God himself says "I will put my law in their minds and write it on their hearts. I will be their God, and they will be my people." Each member of the community sits before the Messiah of Israel "according to his dignity (*lĕpî kĕbôdô*)." "Dignity" expressed here means "honor, glory, abundance."[78] Because the community of Qumran saw themselves as "the Poor" (see Chapter One) they were probably not envisioning abundance of riches, but rather abundance of righteousness.

What is fascinating here is that we have another parallel in this event to the Last Supper of Jesus. At this Last Supper of Jesus, the disciples were arguing over their "position" at the table, causing Jesus to scold them for seeking the seats of honor (Luke 22:24). At this supper, Jesus proclaimed the New Covenant of Jeremiah 31 as the new covenant of his body and blood in all three of the synoptic gospels (Matthew26:28, Mark 14, 24, and Luke 22:20). This New Covenant was again pronounced by Paul in 1 Corinthians 11:25. In Hebrews, Jesus was declared to be the mediator of a New Covenant (Hebrews 9:15-20).

"The Messianic Apocalypse"(4Q521)

In the Messianic Apocalypse, some phrases have apparent similarities to passages from Matthew and Luke. There are also references to a general believer's resurrection from the dead. Though Fitzmyer downplays the significance of the phrase "he will make the dead live"[79] we know from the New Testament that the general resurrection from the dead was an expectation among most Jews (except, perhaps, the Sadducees; cf. Matthew 22:23). It is hard to see what else this phrase might mean. Therefore, I think it is reasonable to see this passage as a reference to the general resurrection of the dead as in Daniel 12:2 in the context of messianic expectation.

Eisenman and Wise point out a continual reference to four "more or less interchangeable allusions and literary self-designations." These include the Righteous (*Zaddikim*), the Pious (*ḥassîdîm*), the Meek (*ʿānāwîm*), and the Faithful (*ĕmŭnim*).[80] The term "Pious" shares the root with (*ḥesed*) which refers to the keeping "covenant and…lovingkindness" of God.[81] So the *ḥassîdîm* are those who are faithful to the covenant of God and by doing so, show "kindness" to God. In the reverse, when God shows *ḥesed* he is being merciful, restraining his judgment because of his covenant love (see Chapter Ten). Therefore, an alternative translation of 4Q521 f2ii line 9: "Forever I trust waiting for His unfailing love (*ḥesed*)"[82] echoes some of the beauty of the Psalms where the psalmist proclaims the covenant mercies and unfailing love of God (Psalms 18:50; 32:10; 51:1 and more).

The context following a command to "listen" or "obey" (*šāmaʿ*)[83] God's Messiah is startling in that it portrays this Messiah as having divine qualities. The following lines further reinforce this by referring to this messianic figure as "Lord" or *adonai* (*ādônay*). In lines 11 and 12 we have the promise that the "glorious things that have not come to pass, *adonai* will do according to his word" and then "He will heal the fatally wounded, make the dead live, and have good news for the *ʿānāwîm*."[84] The *ʿānāwîm* are literally the poor and oppressed,[85] and we can be sure that the Qumran community saw themselves as oppressed by the Temple and Roman authorities. Presumably, the people at Qumran were awaiting the fulfillment of the promise of the Messiah, especially as elaborated in Isaiah 61. They believed that this Messiah would be Lord, would heal those hurt in battle and vindicate the dead with resurrection. Referring to the Messiah as *adonai* is all the more remarkable if we understand that the Qumran writers were Essenes; for as Josephus points out, they would not call any mere man Lord.[86]

11QMelchizedek (11Q13)

11QMelchizedek directly links Isaiah 61:1, understood by both the Qumran community and the early Christians as a messianic prophecy, with Melchizedek mentioned first in Genesis 14:18 and then again in Psalm 110:4. The document states that at the same time liberty is proclaimed to the captives (i.e., the righteous), the "rebels" will be taken captive. These rebels are later in the document identified as spirits of Belial. This Melchizedek is the same as the "messenger that announces peace" (Isaiah 52:7) and is identified in this document as the "anointed one" of whom Daniel spoke (Daniel 9:25, 26 and the messenger in Isaiah 61: 2,3. All of these passages are recognized by Christians and by Jews, at least in the Second Temple period, as messianic. The document also identifies "sons of God" as heavenly beings (i.e., angels) who, along with "men of the lot of Melchizedek"[87] will receive the benefits of atonement (*kôpēr* or *kîppûr*)[88] at the trial of God's judgment.

A sampling of other Qumran documents which speak of atonement include:

CD 3:18, 4:6-7, and 9-10

"But God, in his wonderful mysteries, atoned for their failings and pardoned their sins."

"And the detailed list of their deeds... of holiness. These are the very first for whom God atoned..."

"According to the covenant (*brît*; cf. p. 36) which God established with the very first, in order to atone for their sins, so will God atone for them."[89]

4Q159 f1 2:6
"Concerning ransom: the money of the census which he gives as ransom for his own person will be half a shekel..."[90]

4Q504 f1-2 2:8-10
"You became angry with them in order to destroy them; but you took pity on them in your love for them, and on account of your covenant (*brît*)--for Moses atoned for their sin—and so that they would know your great power and your abundant kindness (*ḥesed*)..."[91]

In the Old Testament the noun *kôpēr* means "ransom" or the exchange of one life for another, and the verb *kîppûr* means "to cover over (propitiate)" or "pacify (expiate)." In all the above selections except for 4Q159, the verb is used. It is difficult to know exactly what is meant by the verb *kîppûr*. Some Old Testament scholars such as Von Rad and Dodd argue that the word is best understood as "to expiate" or "to make null the offending act" whereas others such as Vincent Taylor and Leon Morris argue the meaning is "to propitiate" or "to moderate the attitude of the offended party."[92]

"To expiate" implies that the offended party, God, no longer is able to see the offending act because the offending act has been eliminated by another act; whereas, "to propitiate" means that the offending act is not necessarily eliminated, but somehow compensation has been provided so that the offended party, God, has been placated. In common parlance, "expiation" happens when a runaway nuclear device spewing radiation, while tethered to an individual and slowly killing that individual in the process, is removed at great risk to the remover. Propitiation happens when one finds a large fly in one's soup, a complaint is made, and the waiter brings a new, bug-free soup with a coupon for a free meal presumably at the expense of the restaurant.

In CD 3:18, 4:6-7, and 9-10 and 4Q266, the meaning appears to be "to expiate" where as in 4Q504 Moses is seen as trying to moderate God's actions from anger to kindness. In all passages, the covenant that is referred to is the covenant established by God with Moses on Mount Sinai which included the giving of the Law (Exodus 24:1-8; 19:3-9) and the association with it of blood atonement through animal sacrifice.

11QMelchizedek identifies Melchizedek as a messianic, divine being just as the book of Hebrews does. According to Fitzmyer, Jews puzzled over this figure in that he was declared a priest of God Most High but had no genealogy. This is why he can be said to resemble the Son of God and continue as a priest forever (Hebrews 7:3).[93] In 4QMelchizedek, this Melchizedek will preside at the judgment of God, carry out God's vengeance against Belial, and receive aid from the "gods of justice" (i.e. angels, sons of God) in freeing the captives mentioned in Isaiah 61:1.

This Melchizedek is also identified in this document as the messenger who in Isaiah 52:7 announces peace, salvation and the reign of God. He is also the "anointed of the spirit" mentioned in Daniel 9:25-26 which records the famous messianic prophecy of the 70 weeks. Some have interpreted these verses in Daniel as specifically announcing the time of Messiah's visitation 480 years after the decree of Cyrus.[94] It is also interesting that while many scholars claim that the book of Daniel could not possibly have been written before 165 B.C.E. it is widely quoted as Scripture in Qumran documents by 25 B.C.E. , and Daniel himself is regarded as a prophet.

Indeed, from fragments (one portion alone is dated to 125 B.C.E.) found in the Qumran caves, scholars can construct almost a complete book (up to eleven chapters, and more from various *pēšārîm*).[95] It is indeed surprising that many scholars still hold on to the 165 B.C.E. date for its authorship. This would mean that Second Temple era Jews were regarding a forgery purported as authored by Daniel in the Sixth Century B.C.E. to be Scripture just 40 years after it was written! It would seem more rational to understand that Daniel was available to Ezra in some form during his reform of the canon in 458 B.C.E. (see Chapter Eleven).

It may be a bit presumptuous to regard this community at Qumran as Christian, but it is conceivable that from the language used, these people were prepared to receive Jesus as Lord and Messiah and could have made up a large part of the early converts to Christianity in Jerusalem. Not only might they have made up the bulk of the non-hellenized Jews in the church in Jerusalem, but they may have been the driving force behind the "judaizers" mentioned by Paul in Galatians (see Chapter Two).

"Son of God" "Son of the Most High"

In Luke 1:32, 35 the angel Gabriel tells Mary, who has conceived a child through God, that this son "will be great and be called the Son of the Most High." Jesus is referred to as Son of God (*theou huios*) first by John the Baptist (John 1:34) and Nathaniel (John 1:49), then by the Devil (Matthew 4:3, 6; Luke 4:3, 9, Luke 8:28), then by demons (Matthew 8:29; Mark 3:11, 5:7; Luke 4:41), and finally by those in the boat after He stilled a storm (Matthew 14:33). The title "Son of God" is also used by Martha of Jesus at the raising of Lazarus (John 11:27) and by Peter in reference to Jesus (Matthew 16:16). The title is also used in a mocking fashion, first by the high priest (Matthew 26:63; Luke 22:7; cf. John 19:7), then by the crowd at the cross (Matthew 27:40, 43). Finally, the centurion at the cross thoughtfully wonders if Jesus may truly be the "Son of God" (Matthew 27:54, Mark 15:39).

Jesus also refers to himself as the "Son of God" in the third person (John 5:25) and John in his gospel makes the observation that Jesus is the "Son of God" (John 20:31) and again in his epistles (1 John 3:8, 4:15, I John 5:5, 9-20, 2 John 1:9) and in Revelation (2:18). After Pentecost, the apostles preach Jesus as the "Son of God" (Acts 9:20). The title "Son of God" for Jesus seemed to be a favorite of Paul (Romans 1:4, Romans 8:3, 29; 2 Corinthians 1:19; Galatians 2:20, 4:4, 6; Ephesians 4:13). The book of Hebrews designates Jesus as "Son of God" (4:14, 6:6, 10:29) and alludes to this title with references in Psalms 2:7, 12 (Hebrews 1:8, 5:5). In Hebrews 7:3 the mysterious Melchizedek, first mentioned in Genesis 14:8 and again in Psalm 110:4 where he is called an eternal priest (cf. Hebrews 7:17), is referred to as like the "Son of God."

In the Old Testament, other than a reference to mysterious angelic beings in Job 1:6, 2:1, and, according to some, Genesis 6:4 ("sons of God" see Chapter Six), and the passages referred to above in Psalms 2, the only mention of God having a Son with divine characteristics is Isaiah 9:6. For many years, it was believed by many scholars that the New Testament phrase "Son of God" was a Hellenistic term applied to Jesus by gentile converts to Christianity; it could not possibly have come from Palestine was the thinking. Instead, presuppositions of gentile believers who, in their own mythology had demi-gods and sons of gods, prepared them to understand Jesus in like manner.[96]

We know from 4Q246, also known as "The Son of God" text,[97] that this phrase was probably a common expression for Messiah among Second Temple Period Jews even though the word *māšîaḥ* is not found in the text.[98] How do we know this? In 4Q246 the "Son of God" (Aramaic: *bar ēl*) is also referred to as "son of the Most High" (*bar ʿelwôn* or in Hebrew *bēn ʿelwôn*) and these phrases are clearly titles. Verbs of "naming" and "calling" along with the Aramaic *ytʾ mr* "he shall be called" make this apparent. The document is apocalyptic and reflects the tone and fervor of Palestinian Judaism.

Fitzmyer points out that the use of the word *ēl* is not found in biblical Aramaic (normally, *ĕlôhîm* would be used; cf. Daniel 3:26 and 4:32 where it is used with *ʿelwôn*). The fact that it is found again in column 2: 4, 7 of 4Q246 would confirm that *ēl* was at least familiar to Palestinian Jews as a name for God. This would help confirm that Jesus' dying words on the cross in Matthew 27:46 would be idiomatic Aramaic and not a problematic combination of Hebrew and Aramaic as once thought.[99]

The two messiahs, one a king and the other a priest, mentioned in the Manual of Discipline and CD are not mentioned here. Fitzmyer argues successfully that this messiah is a kingly and not a priestly messiah. This "Son of God" will have a kingdom that is eternal and his ways are truth and judgment. The writer appears to be referencing Psalms 72:1-2 and Psalm 110:4-6. In the Psalm 72 passage, the psalmist references Solomon, son of David as judge over Israel. We know from other Qumran texts, particularly 4Q252 (4QGenesis *pēšer*), that the Messiah was understood to be a descendent of David.[100] The early church also saw Jesus' descent from David as crucial to identifying Him as Messiah (genealogies of Matthew 1 and Luke 3; Romans 1:3).

However, unlike Jesus and his Kingdom, at least initially, the kingdom of the Dead Sea Scrolls is a warlike kingdom which wars against the peoples, presumably those that oppress Israel. The Qumran messiah physically overthrows the Gentiles occupying the land, whereas the New Testament messiah, Jesus, will establish a kingdom that is not of this world (John 18:36). The Psalm 110 passage links the eternal Melchizedek with the judgment of God. We know from our discussion of 11QMelchizedek (see

Chapter Four) that Melchizedek was seen by the Qumran community, and by implication first century Jews in general, as messianic. The conclusion of Elaine Pagels in her book *Beyond Belief*, that the titles "son of God" and "messiah" at the time of the destruction of the Qumran community only designated "human roles," is not borne out by the facts.[101]

Though there is a difference between the messianic views of Qumran and those of the New Testament, we can surmise at the very least that Palestinian Jews contemporary with Jesus were familiar with the messianic fervor of the Qumran community or communities like them, and were expecting such a war-like messiah in light of the oppression from Rome. When Jesus fed the five thousand, the people present saw this as a sign that their messianic expectations were about to be fulfilled and they sought to force him to be their king (cf. John 6:14).

Though Jesus may have been a disappointment as Messiah to people like those from Qumran, he was also no demi-god to the early church. The titles attributed to him (Mediator, Messiah, Son of God) are definitely anchored in the Old Testament.

Jesus the God-Man

The word for mediator (*mesitēs*) in the Hellenistic world means "a guarantor" or something like our modern day "umpire."[102] A mediator is a neutral that both sides can trust. However, the writer of Hebrews is probably drawing from the Old Testament concept of "intercessor" unrelated previously with the word (*mesitēs* is not found in the LXX).[103] This becomes clear when we observe the reference to Moses in Hebrews 1:19. Christ acts as one whom, on our behalf before God, "buys us back" to God by his death.

In 1 Timothy 2:4-5, it is clear that God's intention is to save. "This demands the thought of the singularity and uniqueness of God and the Mediator."[104] That is both God, the party at odds with man, and the mediator between God and man, are one and the same. The fact that He is also man brings us full circle to the doctrine of the God-Man. The concept of God and mediator being one and the same finds its precedent in Job (16:18-22). Job identifies God as the party at odds with him (18:21), but understands God as a witness to testify on Job's behalf!

44

The Eternity and Nature of the Logos

Matthew 24:35→Isaiah 40:8. Jesus <u>is</u> the Logos (John 1:1) of God. The Logos is declared eternal in plural form in the Matthew passage. Compare with 1 Peter 1:23—"the Logos of God abides forever." Compare again with Hebrews 13:8 – "Jesus Christ the same yesterday, today and forever." There are two words in Greek for "word": *rhēma* focus on the speech itself as a vessel; and *logos* "focus on the expression of a thought that the speech contains. Jesus is the perfect expression of God's thoughts.

Attributes of God as Applied to Jesus

<u>God is life</u>. John 5:26→John 1:4, 14:6 "life" *zōē* is life as only God has it, as opposed to *psuchē* which means "soulish life."

<u>God is light</u>. Psalm 27:1, 1 John 1:5→John 1:4-9. YHWH is my light, John says Jesus is "the true Light." The Greek word is *phōs* "the essence of light" as opposed to *luchnos* which means, light as seen through an instrument such as a portable lamp (John 5:35).

<u>God is self-existent and eternal</u>. Exodus 3:14→John 8:58. By no means can *egō eimi* be translated "I have been." Jesus is applying the name of the Eternal Existing One, YHWH God, to Himself. Why else would the horrified Jews try to stone Him to death!

<u>God is Truth</u>. Titus 1:2→John 14:6. This claim on the part of Jesus <u>must</u> cause a reaction on the part of those that truly hear it!

Titles Given Both Jesus and YHWH

<u>Bridegroom</u>. Mark 2:19, Matthew 25:1-3→Isaiah 62:5, Hosea 2:16.

<u>Good Shepherd</u>. Psalm 23:1, Ezekiel 34:15→John 10:11, 1 Peter 2:25, Hebrew 13:20.

<u>Savior.</u> Isaiah 43:3→Acts 5:31. In the Isaiah passage, vs. 11 and 12, YHWH is declared the <u>only</u> savior.

<u>Philippians 2:10</u>→Isaiah 45:21-23. In the Isaiah passage, YHWH God is emphasizing His Unity—there is none other to share His absolute

sovereignty. However, in the Philippians passage, a Jew familiar with this Old Testament passage quotes the passage almost verbatim and applies it to Jesus. If Jesus were not YHWH, this would be nothing short of blasphemy!

CHAPTER SIX: Who are the "Sons of God" in Genesis 6:4?

The identification of the "sons of God" in Genesis 6:4 as fallen angelic beings has been widely popularized in Christian evangelical and Pentecostal circles by Chuck Missler.[105]   Recently, a more scholarly argument, proposed by Ronald S. Hendel, uses findings from the Dead Sea Scrolls to argue that a fragment of Deuteronomy 32:8 clearly shows the Hebrew *běnê ēlîm* to be "sons of God" instead of "sons of Israel" as in the Masoretic text. This gives the text a more mythological flavor. Hendel proposes that this provides evidence that the Genesis 6:4 text should be seen as employing mythological language as well. We also have evidence from 4Q532 and other Qumran documents that the Qumran community interpreted the "sons of God" in Genesis 6:4 as fallen angels.[106]

Other Qumran documents that shed light on the theology of the Qumran community concerning the interpretation of "sons of God" as "fallen angels" include the so-called "Book of Giants" (1Q23, 4Q203, 4Q530, 4Q531, and 6Q8). In these and other documents found at Qumran, the *běnê ēlîm* or *běnê ělôhîm* are synonymous with the "Watchers" (angelic beings who sire the giants, cf. Chapter Seven) and the *něpilîm* are synonymous with "Giants" (*gbrye*). The Hebrew root for the Aramaic *gbrye* '"mighty" is used to describe actions of God whether in judgment (Genesis 7:18) or love (Psalm 103:11). It is used in 2 Samuel 1:23 to describe the strength of Saul and Jonathan as warriors. In Psalm 65:3, the word is used to describe being "overwhelmed by sins." The segolate form *geber* is used in Exodus 10:11, 12:37, Joshua 7:14-17 and Isaiah 22:7 to describe men doing masculine work (such as warfare--as opposed to women and children) presumably because they have the strength to do it.

Of course, if we are to understand the Genesis 6:4 text as speaking of fallen angels who have intercourse with women we have a clear contradiction with Luke 20:35, 36 which says in the resurrection, we neither marry or are given in marriage, but are like the angels. Now if our condition in resurrection is "like the angels" then not to marry or be given in marriage (i.e. not having sexual intercourse) is the condition. One could argue that this does not preclude the *possibility* of sexual intercourse, but then one must wonder why Luke would mention this in the first place if that is not what is meant.

"Sons of God" as a clear title of angels (or at least heavenly beings) is found in Job 1:6, 2:1 and 38:7. Mention is also made in Psalm 29:1 (*bĕnē ēlîm*) where the phrase is translated "mighty ones" in the NIV. Clearly, heaven is seen as the realm of God and other beings who present themselves to and converse with God. The reference is to godly beings which naturally have an audience with God. However, Satan is referred to as separate from this group. So, if the term "sons of God" is simply a synonym for angelic beings, then why is Satan or Lucifer, who is also an angelic, though fallen, being (Isaiah 14:12) distinct? Perhaps the term does not refer to angelic beings at all, but instead to beings both heavenly and human who "walk with God." This might explain the reference in Luke 3:37 that Adam was a "son of God" in that he walked with God.

Missler's attack on the Scofield bible reference to Isaiah 43:6 further confirms my point. Isaiah 43:6 "my sons and daughters" is another way of saying "sons of God" and "daughters of God" or Old Testament believers. Other Old Testament references to "sons of God" or "children of God" refer to believers. Deuteronomy 32:5 and Psalm 73:15 allude to "his sons" with the pronoun antecedent "God," all the while referencing people in the context (cf. also, Deuteronomy 14:1 and Hosea 1:10). All of these references refer to the "sons of God" as Old Testament believers. Genesis 6:4 should be included among the other texts mentioned here as referencing godly believers.

It is best to understand the sons of God and daughters of men in Genesis 6 as behavioral designations, not physical lines. The sons of God were normally godly men who sinned by inter-marrying with women from ungodly homes. Nephilim, (*nĕpilîm* "giants" or *gigantes* in the Septuagint, see Brown, Driver, Briggs, p. 658), their offspring, simply refers to large "mighty men of valor (*ha gĕbarîm*)" honored as such after their deaths.[107] The emphasis with the use of *nĕpilîm* is on their valor in battle and death, not on their physical stature. The *nĕpilîm* lived before and after the Flood of Genesis, so any physical connection between the pre- and post-diluvial mention would be on the assumption that the original *nĕpilîm* were not killed off by the Flood. The Philistine Goliath probably was a descendent from post-diluvian *nĕpilîm*. There is no textual requirement to understand giants as descendents from a supposed union between angels and humans.

In the early church, Augustine (Sixth Century) and Cyril of Alexandria (Fifth Century) both denied the theory that the "sons of God" in Genesis

6:4 were angelic beings. An even earlier denial of this theory was made by Julius Africanus (late Second to early Third Century) known to us through Eusebius. He was apparently a Hebrew and Greek scholar and church historian concerned with careful exegesis of biblical texts.[108]

The Septuagint translators used the term *hoi gigantes* a form of the word *gigas,* (also used for *nĕpilîm* in the only other reference in Numbers 13:33) which refers to "sons of Gaia", a race of giants destroyed by the gods. If the translators are actually making a reference to this myth, then it only proves the influence that this myth had on the Judaism of the time. It could be that they are using the word simply to translate as "mighty men of valor" or "giants" without a mythical reference. In either case, this does not necessitate acceptance by Christians of pagan myths or rabbinic musings. Missler's entire argument seems to be based on a refutation of physical lines. But I have already pointed out that "sons of God" can refer to godly men as well as angels. The one who knows God and can be called His child is a "son of God" whether in the Old or the New Testament.

According to Missler:

> "In the mouths of two or three witnesses every word shall be established... In Biblical matters, it is essential to always compare Scripture with Scripture. The New Testament confirmations in Jude and 2 Peter are impossible to ignore. For if God spared not the angels that sinned, but cast them down to hell [Tartarus], and delivered them into chains of darkness, to be reserved unto judgment; And spared not the old world, but saved Noah the eighth person, a preacher of righteousness, bringing in the flood upon the world of the ungodly (2 Peter 2:4-5)...Peter's comments even establishes the time of the fall of these angels to the days of the Flood of Noah."

Peter's comments do nothing of the sort! How does Missler get this from the text? There is no reason to see the flood of Noah as a response to the sins of fallen angels. These sins do not even have to be sexual. This is another example of how Missler "tortures the data" of the biblical text (to use one of his terms). Genesis 6:4 does not demonstrate that the *nĕpilîm* mentioned here continued after the flood as some kind of freak race. "After that" does not give a time after the Flood. Only the line of Noah remained after the flood.

Missler refers to Luke 20:36 apparently to prove that angels have bodies. However, the Luke passage says that believers, who will have bodies because of the resurrection, will be like the angels in that they will never die. This does not require the leap that angels also have bodies capable of engaging in sexual intercourse. Though there are references to appearances of angels with bodies that can eat food (Genesis 18), there are no references to angels, fallen or otherwise, engaging in sexual activity with women, unless, of course, one insists on interpreting "sons of God" in Genesis 6:4 as angelic beings.

In 2 Corinthians 5:2 the word "dwelling" means body, something all human beings must have in order to be fully human, and refers to the resurrection. The word as it is used in Jude 6 refers to the place where the angels dwell, that is, heaven.[109] Missler seems to forget that words take their meaning from the context in which they appear. There is no evidence that fallen angels had a body capable of engaging in sexual acts with women and the Jude passage certainly cannot be used to support such an assertion.

Ronald Hendel's article *When the Sons of God Cavorted with the Daughters of Men* takes a similar approach to the identity of the "sons of God" in Genesis 6:4 as Missler, but from a more scholarly perspective. Hendel points to the discovery at Qumran of a Hebrew text of Deuteronomy 32:8 (4QDeut[j]) that refers to "sons of God." The phrase found in this text would agree with the LXX and supplant the text "sons of Israel" used by the Masorites and found also in the Samaritan Pentatuech. It is clear that the text makes more sense if "sons of God" is the correct variant.

The passage says that in times of old, God established the boundaries according to the number of the "sons of God" or heavenly beings. If we take the passage to read "according to the number of the sons of Israel, we have the problem brought out by the question: How does God establish boundaries according to the number of the sons of Israel if Israel did not exist at that time?

While I would agree that the Deuteronomy 32:8 reading "sons of God" was probably the original text, I do not agree that it helps shed light on Genesis 6:4. I have already pointed out that "sons of God" can refer to godly character traits whether displayed in angels or men, and therefore,

50

the "sons of God" in Genesis 6:4 could refer to godly men. I have also pointed out that there is no other allusion or otherwise mention of angels mating with women in the Bible and, in fact, the New Testament seems to discount the possibility (Luke 20:35, 36).

Hendel continues his explanation of Genesis 6:4 by looking for parallels in Ugaritic literature which identify the *banu ili* or *banu ili-mi* or "sons of God" as deities, and the Babylonian Gilgamesh Epic with its parallels in language with Genesis. He does not give us a parallel of gods mating with humans, but uses similarity in language between the Babylonian story and Genesis ("the people multiplied," the destruction of humanity in a flood) to draw his conclusions.

In asserting that Genesis *must* have been influenced by the Babylonian story, Hendel feels that the writer of Genesis apparently left vestiges of Babylonian mythology in the text. Just as the Babylonian flood was the result of a "cosmic imbalance" of overpopulation, the Genesis 6:4 text was originally a story of a cosmic imbalance brought on by sex between gods and women. According to Hendel the Genesis account tries to cover up, unsuccessfully, this original understanding and attributes the Flood in Genesis to sin—rebellion against God.

However, why do we have to assume that Genesis 6:4 is an import from Babylon or influenced by the Canaanites of Ugarit? When Abraham came into the land of Canaan, he undoubtedly knew of the original flood story and its corruption by the Babylonians. He took over the words for God (*ĕl*, *ĕlôhîm*) and recast "sons of God" as godly beings, heavenly or human. Like modern missionaries, he was trying to find something in the Canaanite context that would help him communicate about his God, Yahweh (*YHWH*). For example, when Jesuit missionaries went to China in the Sixteenth Century they wrestled with what word in the Chinese language should be used for "God" and ended up adopting the term *shang di* or "above the emperor," a term also used by Confucius to describe God.[110] This does not mean that these missionaries were also importing Chinese mythological concepts of gods. Instead they were simply using language in a new way.

Following the assumption that all facts available to the unbiased researcher have been thoroughly researched, we conclude that although the phrase "sons of God" *could* linguistically be understood as angels or heavenly beings in Genesis 6:4, it does not *have to* be understood as such. If an *interpretation* of a passage does damage to the overall theology and unity of Scripture then this interpretation must be suspect. In the words of John Warwick Montgomery in regard to forming a proper hermeneutic, we should never allow an outside source to master Holy Scripture:

> "Extra-biblical linguistic and cultural considerations must be employed ministerially, never magisterially, in the interpretation of a text; and any use of extra-biblical material to arrive at an interpretation inconsistent with the veracity of the scriptural passage is to be regarded as magisterial and therefore illegitimate. Extra-biblical data can and should put questions to a text, but only Scripture itself can in the last analysis legitimately answer questions about itself."[111]

Those who hold to a high view of Scripture can make use of Ugarit and Babylon to help in understanding a biblical text, but never at the expense of an understanding of the unity and authority of Scripture.[112]

CHAPTER SEVEN: Angels and Watchers

The O. Testament term for angels usually translated as *angeloi* in the LXX is *malĕ'āk*. In the Pentateuch and Joshua, the term is associated directly with YHWH, and the reference is to "the angel of the Lord." When the term is by itself it can refer to a human being as a messenger (e.g., 1 Kings 19:2) or to a supernatural "angel" as a messenger (e.g., 1 Kings 19:5).

Many scholars see virtually no angelology in the older books and a well-defined angelology in what they consider to be exilic and post-exilic literature. Hans Bietenhard says that in the more recent literature there is a pronounced angelology with various hierarchies serving and praising God in the heavenly realm (e.g., Job 1:6 and Isaiah 6:2f), but in the older literature "angels" do not have this role. In the post-exilic literature, angels are not always specifically referred to as *malĕ'āk*, but often as "...'holy ones', 'strong ones', 'heroes', 'sons of God'..." They are beings that interact in specific instances between men and God.[113]

Whereas Bietenhard sees a more pronounced appearance of these beings in post-exilic literature, Von Rad sees a frequent appearance of these beings in pre-exilic literature. When Jacob has his dream of heavenly beings ascending and descending the ladder (Genesis 28) the term used for these beings is *bĕnê ĕlôhîm* not *malĕ'āk*, but they are surely synonymous. Von Rad also understands the Book of Job as being pre-exilic and that book also uses *bĕnê ĕlôhîm* not *malĕ'āk* for these beings.[114]

In Deuteronomy 33 and Psalm 68 we have implicit references to angelic involvement in the giving of the Law. This belief was also widespread among the rabbis and was mentioned by Josephus in his *Antiquities of the Jews* (discussed later in the chapter). Here, the heavenly beings involved are not called *malĕ'āk* but *qōdeš*.

Deuteronomy 33:2. "The Lord delivered the Law with a myriad (10,000) of 'holy ones' (Heb. *qōdeš*; LXX *angeloi* "angels") from His right hand." Throughout the Old Testament, *qōdeš* is usually translated "holiness" or the essential nature of that which is separated from, even antithetical to that which is common or profane, for the service of God (cf. Leviticus 10:10 and Ezekiel 42:14).[115] The LXX even includes the Greek transliteration of the Hebrew word for Holy One. "Kadēs" is a non-translated proper name.[116] The idea is that the angels were separated for

53

the service of God and intimately involved in the delivery of the Law to the people through Moses.

Psalms 68:17. "The chariots of God comes with thousands of thousands; the Lord (*adonai*) comes as at Sinai *among the holy ones* (*ba qōdeš* -- emphasis mine).

In other words, God has an army of heavenly beings that are in His service. They were instrumental in the giving of the Law on Mt. Sinai and they remain in His service. Quite possibly, these angelic beings may have been the ones Jesus of Nazareth was making reference to in the garden of Gethsemane (Matthew 26:53) when, at the time of His arrest, He said to the companion that had struck the servant of the high priest: "Do you not think I cannot call on my Father, and He will at once put at my disposal twelve legions of angels." This is indeed a reference to the myriads (10,000's) of angels at God's hand (Deuteronomy 33:2).

Angels at Qumran

The word translated "angels" in the Qumran literature includes *malĕʾāk* and its cognates (*malĕʾākî, malĕʾākîm, malĕʾākô,* and *malĕʾākāyw*). *Malĕʾāk* can be read with significant examples in CD16:5, 1QS, 1QM, 4Q177, 4Q216, 4Q286, 4Q369, 4Q495, and 11Q11. *Malĕʾākî* can be found in CD2:6, CD15:17, 1QS, 1QSa, 1QM, 1QHa, 4Q216, 4Q225, 4Q285, 4Q287, 4Q289, 4Q387, 4Q390, 4Q403, 4Q405, 4Q418, 4Q473, 4Q491, 4Q495, 4Q510, 4Q511, 4Q513, 6Q18 and 11Q10. *Malĕʾākîm* can be found in 1QM, 4Q180, 4Q504. *Malĕʾākô* can be found in 4Q434. *Malĕʾākāyw* can be found in 4Q185, 4Q392, 4Q491, 11Q5, 11Q11.

CD2.6. For those who fail to repent (*kpr*; cf. "note 92"), but turn aside (*šûb*) from the path of following His precepts, God will loose His angels of destruction (*hebel*)[117] upon them.

CD15.17. Those with mental or physical defects, or are underage may not enter the congregation because the holy angels are among the congregants (*bĕtôkēkem*; in their midst).

CD16.5. This passage quotes from Deuteronomy 23:23 concerning the responsibility of the confessor to follow through on vows. The one returning to the law of Moses will discover that the angel of Mastemoth has left off from following him.

1QS. Those walking in darkness and evil will be judged by the hands of the angels of destruction (*ḥebel*). Evil doers will come under the authority of the Angel of Darkness (Belial?) who causes them to continue in the paths of darkness.

1QSa. See CD2.6.

1QM. God will overcome with his hand all angels of destruction linked to Belial, the angel of malevolence, made for the pit (1QM1:15, 13:12). Those going into battle must be ritually pure without a physical limitation "because of the holy angels" (*kî malě'ākî qōdeš*). The phrase "because of the angels" appears to be a Semitism used in a Pauline *halakot* (*dia tous angelous*) in 1 Corinthians 11:10. This phrase mentioned here in the War Scroll as well as in the 1 Corinthians passage, would then refer to the authority of the Law as coming through angels. Next, God will send eternal support to the allotted portion (remnant?) of the redeemed (*lěgôral pědôt*) by the power of the majestic angel Michael (1QM17:6). Finally, holy ones and angels (host of angels) will praise God in His holy abode (1M12:1).

1QHa. There is an allotted portion (*běgôral*) who know God's truth and will be judged with compassion. They are joined together in common with the angels.

4Q177. God's angel will remove all sons of light from under the control of Belial.

4Q180. This is a reference to Genesis18 when the three angels appear to Abraham at the oaks of Mamre before the judgment of Sodom and Gomorrah.

4Q185. There is no hope, nor ability to struggle against God's wrath. There is no ability to stand before God's holy angels. Column 2:6 seems to imply that neither darkness, nor fog can cover from these angels.

4Q216. Angels minister before the Lord (5:5) and there is a call to rest on the seventh day (Sabbath) with the angels of His presence (before the face of God).

4Q225. This is a commentary on Genesis 22:7-8 when Abraham offers up his son Isaac on an altar of sacrifice. The angels weep at the scene.

4Q285. The holy angels are blessed.

4Q286. A curse upon the angel of the pit and the spirit of destruction

4Q287. This passage speaks of angels of fire and spirits of clouds. They are ministers in their glorious splendor, holy spirits in their glorious dwelling places.

4Q289. The holy angels are among the congregants.

4Q369. In this fragment, angels are described as "angels of your peace" and "angel of intercession" (ʾābôt)[118]

4Q387. God will abandon the land to the angels of Mastemoth.

4Q390. (f1:11) In the seventh jubilee, after the land's destruction, Israel will forget law, festival, Sabbath and covenant. A remnant will escape in order not to be completely destroyed in God's wrath. However, God's face is hidden from them; they shall again do evil, and the angels of Mastemoth will rule over them.

(f2i:7) The rule of Belial will be over them in order to hand them over to the sword for a week of years (šābʿa).[119] On the jubilee, all God's commandments will be in violation and he will give them over into the hands of the angels of Mastemoth who will have dominion over them.

4Q392. God has made winds and lightning…His angels and ministers of the inner sanctuary.

4Q403. An offering of praise to God during the eighth Sabbath sacrifice, the 23rd of the second month—seven priests approach God in the sanctuary where mention is made of the prince, the angels (could be human messengers) of the king in their extraordinary habitation.

4Q405. (f17 and 19). These fragments speak of the angels as angels of power, glory and beauty (f17). The holy angels of God interact with the *debirim* (another class of angels?) in a visual tapestry of worship before holy God.

4Q405. (f20-22) In the worship of God the holy angels are beautifully choreographed moving back as the glorious *ofanim* "wheels" (cf. 4Q403, 11Q17; Ezekiel 1:15f) move forward. Then they emerge again among the *ofanim*. The *ofanim* are apparently another class of angelic beings.

4Q405. (f23) When the "divinities of knowledge" (*'ĕl da'at*) enter in through the gates of glory the holy angels depart to their realms (*memĕšālā*)[120]. In their coming and going both gates (*š'ar*)[121] of exit and entrance declare the glory of the king and bless the spirits coming and going. There is none among them that goes against a precept or regulation of the king (cf. Psalm 100:4)

4Q418. The God of knowledge will establish the ways of those who seek enlightenment. Those who inherit truth become vigilant. There is peace and quiet. The holy angels are in heaven (presumably observing).

4Q434. God has positioned His holy angels near the chosen people.

4Q473. Everyone who does evil will be hit with various plagues of blight, mildew, snow, ice and hail together with all the angels of destruction.

4Q491. Because the holy angels are within the rows in the formation to battle, those not pure will not be able to participate.

4Q495. All the spirits of truth are under the dominion of God. Belial, the enemy angel, was created for the "pit" (cf. Matthew 25:41).[122] The domain of Belial is darkness and his counsel is evil and wickedness. All the spirits with him, angels of Mastemoth, follow darkness.

4Q504. All the angels of the vault of heaven (*rāqî'a*; the expanse or vault of heaven, Genesis1:6)

4Q510. The Instructor proclaims the glorious splendor so as to terrify all the spirits of the destroying angels, spirits of the bastards.

4Q511. The lot of God with the angels of brilliance (luminescence) of God's glory.

4Q513. This document speaks of angelic food.

6Q18. The angels are righteous.

11Q5. All the angels, when they saw the Lord, sang because He showed them things they had not known before.

11Q10. A targum on Job 38:7. The morning stars shine together and all the angels of God shout together. In the Job text the angels of God are the "sons of God" (*běnê ělôhîm*).

11Q11. Evil ones can expect the judgment of God in the form of a mighty angel sent against them. God urges all his angels (to follow Him?)

The word translated "holy ones" (from *qaddîš* and its cognates *qaddîšî, qaddîšîn, qĕdôšô* and Heb. *qaddîšîm*) can be found throughout the Qumran literature. Relating to our discussion: *Qaddîšî* can be found in 4Q201 Col 4:10 and 4Q202f1 Col. 3:11; *Qaddîšîn* can be found in 1Q20, 4Q204, 4Q536; *Qĕdôšô*, can be found in the Damascus Document found at Geniza in 1910 (CD20) and 4Q403; *Qaddîšîm* can be found in 1QHa, 1QM, 1QS, 4Q400, 4Q401, 4Q402, 4Q403, 4Q404, 4Q405, 4Q417, 4Q491, 4Q502, 4Q503, 4Q504, 4Q510 and 4Q521.

1QHa. The worshipper is praising God for his redemption from corruption[123] Transgressions are cleansed that the redeemed might share together with the assembly (*yahad*) of the holy ones.

1QM. This is a description of the inevitable destruction of the *kittîm* (cf. Chapter Eight) or "sons of darkness" by the "sons of light." The sons of light include the people of the land, Judah, Benjamin and Levi, and the assembly of the gods (holy ones or angels). The sons of darkness include all the *kittîm*, the "lot of Belial," Japhet and Ashur, and the congregation of men. It is clear from this document that the angels of God or holy ones, are fighting alongside Israel in the battle against the *kittîm* (Column 12:8).

It is also clear that there are angels that are fighting with Belial and the sons of darkness (Column 13:11-12). Their end is the pit.

1QS. This section of the "Rule of the Community" almost presupposes the apostle Paul in Romans and Galatians with its acknowledgement that *mišĕpāṭ* (justification)[124] comes from God as a result of his *ḥesed* (loving-kindness, cf. Chapter Ten). God chooses to give the righteous his eternal inheritance "in the legacy of the Holy Ones" – a sharing of the assembly on earth with the assembly in heaven.

1Q20. It is clear that the author of this document identifies the "watchers" as "holy ones" identical with the "sons of God" *bĕnē ēlîm* of Genesis 6:4, which we have already identified as believers who have turned away from God to marry unbelieving women (see Chapter Six "Who are the 'Sons of God' in Genesis 6:4"). The author apparently believed in the popular myth of the time that these Nephilim are products of an unholy union between humans and angelic beings.

The Nephilim, also mentioned in the Genesis passage, are mentioned again. According to the author, the offspring of this union "belongs to" (movement towards) these Nephilim. Lamech, the speaker in the passage is concerned that his wife's pregnancy is not from him, but from these Watchers. This Lamech is the son of Methuselah, grandson of Enoch and the conception is apparently that of his son Noah mentioned in Genesis 5:28-29.

4Q201. (1 Enoch 1:1-6) the holy ones are the Watchers. See previous discussion under "Watchers."

4Q202. In Column 3, the "holy ones" appear to be heavenly beings not identified with the Watchers in the rest of the document.

4Q204. (1 Enoch106:13-107:2) The holy ones are they that have shown the author from the tablets of heaven (a reference to the angelic host responsible for giving the Law to Moses on Mt. Sinai).

4Q400. Holy ones mentioned here are the priests separated for service unto the Lord. There are references in Column 2 to a council of the gods or divine beings.

<u>4Q401</u>. God is "King of the gods." The "holy ones of the holy ones" praise God's glory. Song of the Sabbath: this Sabbath is the fourth Sabbath (twenty-fifth of the first month). The Qumran community apparently counted the first month from Nisan (March-April) because they understood that the Creation took place in the spring (cf. note 137), so this would make this Sabbath the second week of April.

<u>4Q402</u>. Fragment 1 is incomprehensible. Fragment 4 was completed from a copy found at Masada. The "gods" are positioned to fight in the war of the heavens.

<u>4Q403</u>. This document, called by scholars "Song of the Sabbath Sacrifice" because of its continual referencing of various Sabbaths throughout the year, is reminiscent of the New Testament Book of Revelation, with its mention of "seven stars" or angels (Revelation 1:20), "seven spirits" (Revelation 4:5) and the Old Testament book of Ezekiel with mention of the *ofanim* (cf. 4Q405, 11Q17).

The third of the sovereign princes[125] celebrates seven times with seven exaltations—a psalm of praise to the Powerful One above all the gods. This Powerful One has seven powers. The second among sovereign princes will bless all that celebrate the King. The third of the sovereign princes blesses in the name of the exalted King. The fourth of the exalted princes will bless all who conduct themselves in a straightforward manner. He will establish majesty with his words. The fifth of the exalted princes will bless all those who "know the mysteries of purity;"[126] those that hasten to do God's will. The sixth sovereign prince will bless those powerful in intellect and who are travelling on a "perfect path."[127] The seventh sovereign prince will bless the "holy ones" (*qĕdôšô*) who make the foundation of knowledge (i.e., the Law; a reference to the participation of the Watchers in the giving of the Law to Moses on Mt. Sinai). He will bless those who exalt the precepts with words (*dobor*) that would make for sturdy shields (*mogēn*; 1 Kings 14:27, Psalm 84:10; cf. Ephesians 6:16). Then, the seven sovereign princes together will bless the God of the "holy ones" (*qĕdôšô*). They will also bless those destined to justice. The next Song of the Sabbath is for the seventh Sabbath or sixteenth of the month.

In Column Two, the gods are in the form of embers of fire. They are also called "spirits of the gods." In the *debir* ("holy of holies" or dwelling place of God, cf. 1 Kings 6:5), the *ofanim* along with the *cherubim* praise together wonderfully.

Line 18 begins with "For the instructor a song" (*lamaśĕkîl šîr*; Psalm 55:1, a *maskil* is a literary term used for musical instruction). This marks the song of the eighth Sabbath sacrifice (the twenty-third of the second month: mid-May?). The eternal "holy ones" (*qĕdôšô*) are called upon to praise God.

4Q404. Divine beings are praising God.

4Q405. Fragments 3-21 apparently are another copy of the Song of the Sabbath Sacrifice. Fragments 21-22, line 6 begin with "A song for instruction" for the twelfth Sabbath (twenty-first of the third month) and announces that the *cherubim* lie prostrate before the God of knowledge and bless when they rise up. Other *ofanim* move forward as the "holy angels" (*mal'ĕkî qaddîš*) move back. They emerge with chariot wheels (*galĕgal*) with the likeness of fire, the spirits of the holy of holies (*qôdeš qodošîm*).

4Q417. The nature of Enosh (son of Seth, Genesis 4:26) was patterned after the holy ones.

4Q491. Here is a reference to a multitude of holy ones in heaven, angels in the very abode of God praising His name.

4Q495. Belial was created for the "pit." Other spirits, angels of destruction, share his lot (cf. 1QM).

4Q502. Initiates, or those reaffirming their membership in the community, also join with the holy ones. This could be a reference to a heavenly or community council.

4Q503. God's name is praised among the holy ones. This could also be a reference to a heavenly or community council.

4Q504. Here we have a brief mention of the holy ones that could be a reference to a heavenly or community council.

4Q510. God is Lord of the holy ones.

4Q521. This appears to be a reference to the giving of the Law on Mount Sinai. All heaven and earth will listen to God's Messiah ("anointed one" Heb. *māšiaḥ*) and not turn away from the commandments of the holy ones.

4Q536. (Aramaic) There is very little context here. Wise, Abegg, and Cook translate this as "he will call to mind the holy angels."[128]

CD20:8. This is a reference to one who would try to join the congregation, but has betrayed the Law—he is lacking in pure obedience. He is "inflicted with a curse by the holy ones (angelic beings) of the Most High." Perhaps this is a reference to a council of angels through whom the law was given to Moses (Deuteronomy 33:2).

The Watchers in the Old Testament

In Daniel 4: 13, 17, and 23 (NIV), King Nebuchadnezzar recounts a dream in which a "messenger" or "holy one" came down from heaven and the decision (i.e., to turn Nebuchadnezzar into a madman) is announced by "messengers" or "holy ones" or "watchers" (NAS). The Aramaic for "watchers" is *ʿîrîn*.[129] It is synonymous with *qaddîšîn* appearing in the book of Daniel (4:5-9) when Nebuchadnezzar says that Daniel "has the spirit of the holy gods" (*rûaḥ ʾēlohîn qaddîšîn*) in him.[130]

The Watchers at Qumran

The word translated "watchers" (*ʿîrîn*) at Qumran can be found at 1Q20 2:1, 16, 4Q201, 4Q203, 4Q206, 4Q212, 4Q530, 4Q531, and 4Q532. Another form, *ʿîrî*, can be found at 4Q202 Columns 2 and 4, 4Q204 Column 6.

1Q20. See previous discussion under "Angels at Qumran."

4Q201. Unlike Daniel, the author of this document (the book of Enoch) appears to hold the Watchers in low esteem. God himself will descend to the earth, walk to Mt. Sinai (a re-affirmation of the importance of the Law in the scheme of things) appear with a great army (of angels?) to punish the Watchers. The language is apocalyptic with peaks melting and mountains flattening reminiscent of language in Isaiah 40:3-5 (cf. Luke 3:4-6).

62

4Q202. In this passage, as in Genesis 6:4, the Watchers are the sons of heaven (sons of God), evil beings who mate with human women. The Watchers have individual names and they were successful in their venture. In extant copies of 1 Enoch, their offspring are giants 3,000 cubits tall (in 4Q202, the text is missing) and had a rapid growth rate. Apparently, other men were their suppliers. When they could not keep up with their supplies, these Watchers sought to kill them. In Column Four (1 Enoch 10:8-12) the King (*more*) commands Gabriel to exterminate (*'ōbēd*, destruction forever) the sons of the Watchers in a war of attrition. Michael is taking the news of the impending destruction of the sons of the Watchers to the Watcher Shemihazah and companions. Absolutely no favor is to be extended to these Watchers. According to Column 6 (1 Enoch 14:4-6) the Watchers will not be allowed to return to heaven. It is here that we can liken these Watchers as fallen demonic beings called the devil's angels in the N. Testament bound for hell and destruction.

4Q203. The sons of the Watchers, or "strong ones" (*gĕborî*) are mentioned in the context of punishment. Shemihaza (the Watcher) and his companions and their wives will be punished with their offspring at the coming of Raphael.

4Q204. Column Five (1 Enoch 10:13-19) contains the text of the judgment of the sons of the Watchers, although the actual mention of the Watchers is missing. In Column Six (Enoch 13:6 to 14:16) the Watchers are mentioned in the text in the context of admonishment.

4Q206. In fragment 1 (1 Enoch 22:3-7) Raphael is called a "Watcher and a holy one" (only called a "holy one" in the R.H. Charles translation from the Ethiopic versions).[131] The narrator asked Raphael about a spirit (*rûah*) that was crying out (*zĕ 'iq*, cf. Daniel 6:21). In fragment three, the Watchers are mentioned without much context. From what can be gathered from the text, it is a portion of 1 Enoch 33:4, which mentions Uriel the "holy angel" (Charles translation) in an apocalyptic situation involving three beasts and portals of heaven with stars (angels?) coming forth.[132]

4Q212. There is a mention of "Watchers" and "holy ones" without much context except that it appears to be from 1 Enoch 93:2 in which Enoch recounts the words that appeared in a heavenly vision, known by the word of holy angels, and learned from heavenly tablets (the Law from Sinai?). The Charles translations says "holy angels."[133]

4Q530. This document discusses a dream of two Giants (*geber*) also called Nephilim who went to the Watcher Shemihazah to tell about their dream. They went to Enoch for an interpretation. The dream was alarming to them. It concerned gardeners watering the roots of a tree. A fire came and burned.

4Q531. The holy ones reside in the heavens. Giants (*geber*) and Nephilim demand much to eat and then destroyed a thing. Perhaps this is a reference to men supplying the Watchers (4Q202) and when the men could not keep up, the Watchers seek to kill them.

4Q532. The Watchers are mentioned in fragment 2, line 7 and are discussed with reference to apparent rape of human women (*ᶜllô* cf. Judges 19:25). This would be, of course, a reference to Genesis 6:4. Eisenman and Wise translate the next line "in the end he will perish and die."[134] The end of these Watchers is eternal destruction.

4Q534. In fragment one, Col.2:15, it is not clear if the reference is to "cities" or "Watchers." Wise, Abegg, and Cook translate: "enclosures shall be built, its work will be like the Watchers."[135]

Other References at Qumran

We have already looked (Chapter One) at the "angels of Mastemoth" in 4Q387 and 4Q390 identified with the "rule of Belial" in 4Q390f2. The "rule of Belial" is also mentioned in 1QS 2:19, 4Q290 f1:2, and 5Q13 f4:4. In 1QS and 5Q13, the "rule of Belial" is tied in with the current evil age. The current age is under the authority of Belial, or as we identified in Chapter One, Satan. Though these "angels of Mastemoth" are not explicitly identified with the Watchers in the Qumran literature, the nature of these beings would identify them as all being in the category of fallen angelic beings.

11Q13. Also known as 11QMelchizedek, this document has already been discussed in Chapter Four. Melchizedek, as portrayed in Genesis and Psalm 110, is an earthly king, but is portrayed in 11Q13 as a heavenly being equated with God (*elohim*) Himself. Melchizedek executes judgment on the "spirits of Belial" (Psalm 82:1) and offers atonement for all the "sons of God" and the men of the lot of Melchizedek on the Day of Atonement at the end of the tenth jubilee (cf. Leviticus 25).[136]

11Q17. This is a litany of praise to God. The scene is a wonderful tapestry of living holy angels blessing their King. The song of praise is the sacrifice of the twelfth Sabbath (twenty-first of the third month). In the presence of God there is a lighted vault filled with praise. Angelic beings are blessing and praising God. These "holy ones" have made some sort of sacrifice involving libations.

Conclusion: Angels at Qumran

There are several things that can be concluded about angels at Qumran. First, there are several different classes of angels. Whereas the O. Testament speaks of several groupings: cherubim, seraphim, the Watchers (in the book of Daniel) and, perhaps the *ofanim*, or the "wheels" of the book of Ezekiel; the Qumran community speaks of all these groupings with express force and frequency, and adds other groups: the *debirim*, angels of destruction (generally regarded as fallen angels, but who fulfill God's purposes in judgment), angels of peace, angels of intercession, angels of the vault of heaven, and angels of luminescence. While it may be premature to understand all these different angels as classes or separate orders in heaven, it is clear that angelic beings in the Qumran angelology had specific tasks and functions.

Also, the Watchers of Qumran were decidedly evil beings and clearly identified with the sons of God mentioned in Genesis 4 who mated with human women to produce grotesque offspring. It is curious that the only mention of Watchers in the O. Testament is in Daniel where they are depicted as benign—not identified with fallen beings.

The angels in Qumran angelology form a council or assembly (*yahad*) that work God's purposes as a group. For example, they provide the Law to Moses on Mt. Sinai, interact in intricate choreography to praise God, and fight alongside the sons of light, or human armies of God in bringing judgment to evil doers. The community at Qumran seems to be set up as a human assembly to picture the assembly in heaven much as the temple in Jerusalem was seen as a depiction of the dwelling of God in heaven.

Finally, the fallen angels appear very developed in Qumran angelology. It appears that Belial is seen as the leader of the fallen angels identified as Satan in the N. Testament. In fact, Mastemoth from the "angels of Mastemoth" (foot soldiers in Belial's army of fallen angels), has a similar Hebrew stem *stm* as Satan, as we have seen earlier (Chapter One). The angels of Mastemoth are always associated with the dominion, or rule of Belial. The N. Testament also speaks of the present evil age as being under the dominion of Satan or Belial (2 Corinthians 4:4, 6:15; cf. Matthew 4:1-11 and Luke 4:1-13).

Angels in the New Testament

The angelology of the N. Testament arose, at least in part, within the Palestinian environment shared with the Qumran community. For example, heavenly beings named Gabriel and Michael (Michael is known as an archangel in the N. Testament), first appear in the book of Daniel. This book and these heavenly beings are also featured prominently in the Qumran documents.

The angel Gabriel plays a prominent role in the gospel of Luke as the "angel of the Lord" (*angeloi theou*) at the annunciation of the birth of Jesus (Matthew's gospel only refers to him as *angeloi theou*). Michael appears in the book of Jude (who also quotes from the extra-biblical book of Enoch, portions of which were found at Qumran) and Revelation.

We have seen that the Watchers are angelic beings that are viewed in a positive light in Daniel. It is interesting that at Qumran, these Watchers are largely portrayed in a negative light. They are fallen beings who roam the earth interfering in the affairs of men and are probably the same sort of beings referred to in the N. Testament as the devil's angels (Matthew 25:41).

In Luke's gospel (Luke 4), Jesus at Nazareth was rejected as a prophet after reading from Isaiah 61:1 and 2 in the synagogue. This passage was known to be prophetic and messianic in the Second Temple Period as both the N. Testament and the Qumran community viewed the passage in this way (cf. 4Q521, 11Q13). Only Moses was also understood by the Qumran community to be a herald of good news (4Q377).

Immediately following this rejection, Luke's narrative has Jesus *confirmed* as a prophet in the light of Isaiah 61 through his exorcisms in Capernaum on the Sabbath. One of the exorcisms involved the mother-in-law of Peter who had a high fever. The text simply says that Jesus "rebuked (seriously warned) the fever" (*epetimēsen tō puretō*). We must understand this as not merely a healing but as an exorcism[137] as the demonic element was addressed. We also know that at Qumran a document of exorcisms (4Q560) names a fever demon, a chills demon, a chest pain demon, a male wasting demon and a female wasting demon. This appears to confirm that at least at Qumran and in the case of Jesus of Nazareth, Second Temple Jews in Palestine understood various diseases such as fever to have demonic origins.

The Scriptural witness to the role of angels in the giving of the Law of God at Mt. Sinai is suggested in the Old Testament passages of Deuteronomy 33:2 and Psalms 68:17, and stated explicitly in the New Testament, in Acts 7:53, Galatians 3:19 and Hebrews 2:2.

Acts 7:53. The Acts passage reads "You have received the Law through the direction or command of angels (*eis diatagas angelōn*)."[138] While the deacon Stephen drives home the culpability of the Jews in their rejection of first the prophets and then their messiah, he states the role of the angels in the giving of the Law on Mt. Sinai.

Galatians 3:19. The Greek phrase, *diatageis di' angelōn en cheiri mesitou*,[139] can be translated (with the ablative and dative of instrument) as "through the command of angels by means of a mediator." In other words, the angels were passing on the law from God through a mediator [Moses] and then to Israel. From Paul's perspective, the law is inferior to the promise as made to Abraham because it passed through subordinates and mediators; whereas, the promise was direct.

Hebrews 2:2. The passage in Hebrews says that God spoke the unalterable word (the giving of the Law on Mt. Sinai) as a melody and used the intermediate agency of the angels (*di' angelōn*) to proclaim it.

Josephus uses the word *angelos* to reference a human messenger in *Ant. 7.249*, but also uses *angelos theios* (angel of God) in *Ant. 4.108* with reference to the angel of the Lord that blocked Baalam's path. Josephus also follows Jewish tradition when he intimates that it was angels that brought the law to Israel (*Ant. 15.136*).[140]

There is also a curious passage in 1 Corinthians 11:10 "For this reason, and because of the angels…" The passage is a Pauline *halakot* (admonition) to the congregants at the church in Corinth. Women are to pray and prophesy with their heads covered (either with long hair put up or some veil).[141] In the ancient world, this would show appropriate respect to the authority of her husband and thus recognize the order of creation. If we understand that the angels were involved in the giving of the Law on Mt. Sinai, then we can also understand "because of the angels" to be a recognition of the angelic involvement in the giving of the Law especially with reference here to the seventh commandment (Exodus 20:14).

1 Thessalonians 4:15-17

This stone (measuring 2.43x1 meters) believed to be part of the Second Temple was excavated by Benjamin Mazar at the southern foot of the Temple Mount. The Hebrew inscription reads: "*To the Trumpeting Place.*" (Wikipedia)

Paul presents the *parousia* as an imminent event. His words reflect the apocalyptic flavor of the Second Temple period, including that of the literature at Qumran. Paul declares the Lord descending (*katabēsetai* Future Middle Indicative, third singular of *katabinō*) from heaven to affect His own purposes. He comes with the voice of an archangel (probably Michael, who is mentioned in the book of Jude as an archangel) and with the trumpet of God.

After the dead are raised, the living are caught up together with the dead in the clouds (*en nephelais*). When Jesus was taken up "into heaven," a cloud (angel) hid him from the view of the disciples (Acts 1:9). This account is followed immediately by two men in white (angels) exhorting the disciples that this Jesus would return in the same way they saw Him go into heaven.

God's presence was accompanied by clouds when He met with Moses on Mt. Sinai. In 4Q287 f2:4, angels are associated with fire and clouds.[142] It is possible that the resurrected saints are being joined, both those alive and those who have died, to be with the angels. When Jesus gave his answer to the Sadducees concerning what happens to the saints during the general resurrection, they are told that they will become like the angels in the heavenlies (Mark 12:25). So then the resurrection of the saints changes the physical properties to be more adapted to heavenly existence as the angels are.

Angels in Hebrews

The author of Hebrews opens in the first two chapters condemning "angel worship" among Jews admonishing readers that Jesus has a position far above that of angels. Which group of Jews would the author be referring to other than those Jews of Qumran. Later, a clear line linking these Jews described in Hebrews with the same group of judaizers that plagued Paul's ministry as described in Galatians and Acts, will be set (cf. Chapter Nine). Sufficient to say that the extensive discussion of angels and their elevation of status among the documents at Qumran is quite evident and may have prompted the comments of the writer of Hebrews.

Angels in Revelation

Revelation opens with a reference to seven stars which we learn are the angels of seven churches. Stars are often code for angels in the Qumran literature (cf. 4Q206, 4Q403). In Revelation 4, angels are referenced as "spirits" and "lamps," designations similar to Qumran which speaks of spirits and angels of luminescence (4Q405, 4Q511). The fourth chapter of Revelation also speaks of twenty-four elders and strange living creatures (Ezekiel 1) who are also angels of God. Angels appear throughout the book of Revelation doing God's will particularly concerning judgment.

'Kittim' (*kittîm*) are first mentioned in Genesis 10:4 as one of the descendents of Japhath, Noah's son. The next verse explains that the sons of Javan ("Javan" is also known as Greece) were "maritime peoples." It is probable that verse five is a scribal gloss. That is, a scribe may have copied someone else's notes on verse four into the text. Evidence for this can be found in 1 Chronicles 1:7 where the same reference to the *kittîm* is made without the explanation.[143]

Kittîm are mentioned again in Numbers 24:24, where they are associated with the famous "Star" prophecy of Balaam (v. 17). The reference is also found in Isaiah 23:1,12 and Ezekiel 27:6, where the word "*kittîm*" is translated "Cyprus" in the NIV, and, finally, Isaiah 23:12, Jeremiah 2:10 and Daniel 11:30. It is clear from the biblical records that these people are maritime people coming from the Mediterranean region in the west, probably in association with Greece.[144]

However, in a later time for both Christianity and the Qumran community, extrapolating from the "Star prophecy" of Numbers 24:17, the *kittîm* take on an apocalyptic meaning and refer to the Romans. In Numbers 24:17, the prophecy of the Star and the Scepter comes from the mouth of the seer Balaam, a name associated with wickedness (see Chapter Three) and defiance of the rule of God. "A scepter (*šēbet*)[145] will rise out of Israel." The scepter was originally associated with the shepherd's staff, but it came to mean rod of authority—used for beating and chastisement. The "scepter", in Numbers 24:17 and Genesis 49:10 refers to authority in Israel but in association with the God of Israel. By the Second Temple period, *šēbet* in Genesis 49:10 was seen as messianic because of its association with Judah, from whom David and his line were to come.

The "star" (*kôkāb*) is synonymous with the "scepter." While the scepter refers to a governing authority, the star refers to angelic or heavenly beings. Often these beings are evil (Isaiah 14:12; Amos 5:26). However, in this context the star is associated with God. In Isaiah 14:12 reference is made to a "morning star" that has fallen from heaven. In Revelation 2:28, 22:16 and 2 Peter 1:19, Jesus is the bright and morning star. Clearly, the New Testament writers saw the "star" as referencing a heavenly being and not necessarily a fallen angel. In the case of Revelation 2:28, 22:16 and 2 Peter 1:19 the star must be identified with Numbers 24:17 and not Isaiah 14:12 even though both the Isaiah reference and New Testament references are to a "morning star." In Revelation 2:27-28, we have a clear reference to Numbers 24:17 in conjunction with Psalm 2:9 which, in context with its own reference to a divine Anointed One who is the Son of God, makes this whole presentation messianic and apocalyptic.

"Kittim" at Qumran

Most references to the *kittîm* in the Dead Sea Scrolls occur in the War Scroll (QM). A nearly complete (as best as one can tell) War Scroll was found in Cave One (1QM) and several fragments of it were found in Cave Four. The overall name for the Cave Four fragments is, predictably, 4QM, with the individual fragment names being: 4Q491 (4QM^a), 4Q492 (4QM^b), 4Q493 (4QM^c), 4Q494 (4QM^d), 4Q495 (4QM^e), 4Q496 (4QM^f), 4Q285 (4QM^g), and 4Q471 (4QM^h). In addition, two other fragments identified as being a part of the War Scroll include the "Words of Michael" text (4Q529) and the "Blessings" text found in Cave Eleven (11Q14). Neither of these fragments references the Kittîm. The word *kittîm* also appears in 4Q169 f3, 4Q247 f1, and 4Q554 f2 c3.

In the opening column of the War Scroll, mention is made of *kittîm* of Asshur and the *kittîm* of Egypt. Presumably, these would be references to the Ptolimies of Egypt and the Antiochenes of Syria—Greek rulers descending from two of the four generals who ascended their respective thrones after the death of Alexander the Great. This might make sense if we understand them the way the Old Testament writers understood them toward the close of the Old Testament period (which would roughly correspond to the end of the Persian/beginning of the Greek period). However, the dating of these documents places them in the Roman period. Therefore, it is best to understand these references as code for the Roman armies from the northeast and southwest, respectively. If that is true, then Edom is probably a reference to Herod, the Edomite King of the Jews. The "sons of darkness" and "armies of Belial" are synonymous with the Kittîm.

Toward the end of the War Scroll, beginning in Column Eleven, reference is again made to warfare against *kittîm*. In Column Eleven, *kittîm* is of Asshur or Assyrian legions from Rome. The Qumran writers believed the destruction of these legions was foretold in Isaiah 31:8. In columns fifteen through nineteen, the "King of *kittîm*" is pitted against the High Priest and brother priests and Levites, presumably the priestly members of Qumran (see Chapter Two). The High Priest will take a position in the front of the line to strengthen the hearts of the people in their fight against *kittîm*, and with the blast of a ram's horn, the priests will call for Israel's warriors to finish off the wounded of *kittîm*. When the survivors flee, the holy ones (*qĕdôšîm*) will pursue them and kill them all. Following this great victory, the people of God will celebrate over the dead bodies of *kittîm*. As an aside, there appears to be a parallel with the struggle between Israel and *kittîm* on the one hand, and the angel Michael's struggle for dominance over "the prince of the dominion of evil" (or Belial) and all other heavenly beings (*ĕlîm* cf. 1QM c.17:5-8).

4Q169 consists of three fragments and forms a commentary or *pēšer* on Nahum. Nahum's prophecy originally predicted the demise of Assyria in the Seventh Century. Little is known about him except that he appears to be from Judah. The Nahum *pēšer* completely ignores the background of the book and instead identifies the main characters in more contemporary terms. The sea in Nahum 1:4 represents all *kittîm* which God will eliminate from the face of the Earth. Bashan is also *kittîm* and Carmel is the king of *kittîm*. Fragments three and four, column one, an interpretation of Nahum 2:12-14, specifically identifies *kittîm* as the Romans: "...from Antiochus up to the appearance of the chiefs of *kittîm*."[146]

4Q247 says something to the effect of "[Zed]ekiah king of Judah [reveal] [ ] sons of Levi and the people of the Earth [ ] king [ ] *kittîm*"[147] which seems to be a further discussion of the war of the Levites and priests of Israel (the Qumran community) against *kittîm*. The reference to Zedekiah, King of Judah may be a reference to the messianic line of David.

Finally, the reference to *kittîm* in 4Q554 fragment 2 column 3 is not at all clear. However, it would be reasonable to assume, with all that has been said before, that the reference toward the Kittîm is negative. Others along with *kittîm* including Edom, Moab and the sons of Ammon, do evil to Israel up to a certain moment—and then the text leaves off.

What we discover in all this is the extreme xenophobia against Gentiles harbored by the Qumran community. This has tremendous significance if we are to understand the "judaizers" of Galatians and Acts to be originally from this community (see Chapter Two). Many from this community were as afflicted as John the Baptist when, while in prison, he sent some of his followers to inquire of Jesus if he was indeed "the one who was to come" (Matthew 11:3). Jesus does not at all appear to be the messianic figure of expectation, certainly not of those from the Qumran community who expected a last day conflagration in which all the Kittîm would be wiped off the face of the Earth. Yet, he did seem to be the One in that he performed miracles as described in Isaiah 61 and came from the line of David.

Regardless of whatever doubts were had about Jesus, however, there would be no doubt in the minds of those coming from a "Qumran" point-of-view that Paul as apostle to the Gentiles could not possibly be a true apostle of the Jewish church because he seemed to go against everything that this community represented. If it is true that the "judaizers" came from Qumran via the church in Jerusalem, then this literature leaves no doubt that Paul and these people would be locked in mortal combat.

CHAPTER NINE: The Calendar

In Colossians 2:16, Paul tells us "therefore do not let anyone judge you by what you eat or drink, or with regard to a religious festival, a New Moon celebration or a Sabbath day (NIV)." Who was doing this judging of the Colossian believers? Indications from the text, and from what we know of the Qumran writers from whose ranks these "judges" may have come, they were the judaizers mentioned in Galatians. Along with disputations concerning the "correct" date for religious festivals, these judaizers practiced a "false humility" and a "worship of angels."

As we have already learned (Chapter One), the Qumran writers often designated themselves as "the Poor" and "the Meek," which was an apparent badge of honor to these people. Also, many of the Dead Sea Scrolls contain exhortations against "the angels of Mastemoth" and "Belial." (cf. Chapter One). Perhaps to Paul, such constant referencing these fallen beings may constitute a form of "worship." According to Curtis Vaughn in his commentary on Colossians, the judaizers at Colossae (following the Qumran writers) made these "elemental spirits" (2:8 *stoicheia*) their chief subject matter.[148]

The "angel worship" among these "judaizers," however, was probably more insidious and destructive to the gospel than just a continual referencing of fallen angels. Michael Goulder, in a recent article in *New Testament Studies* notes that the writer of Hebrews "opens with two chapters designed to show angels are inferior to the Son of God."[149] The author of Hebrews, Goulder points out, uses several Old Testament texts to demonstrate that angelic beings and He who would be God's Anointed were not the same. For example, angels are declared mutable beings in Hebrews 1:7-- they are liable to change; whereas, "God's anointed is addressed as God and his throne remains forever (1:8)."

In Hebrews Chapter Two, the author points out, as Goulder reminds us, that the angels are not even close to the level of the Son of God. God's concern is clearly reserved for the Christian, the brothers of His Son— Jesus the one called "Christ" (2:5-10). Goulder specifically uses the term "Jewish Christian" to refer to the group responsible for this pastoral response by the author of Hebrews. In a footnote, he clarifies that this term is reserved for those Gentiles and Jews "who gave importance to Jewish observances (circumcision, Sabbath, food-laws, etc.)."[150] Paul, though ethnically a Jew, was not a Jewish Christian according to Goulder's definition. Of course, this description precisely matches the people Paul writes against in Galatians and Colossians.

These "judaizers," adversaries of both Paul and the writer of Hebrews, later, as we have suggested (Chapter Two), became the Ebionites. According to Irenaeus, the Christology of these Ebionites is the same as that of Cerinthus, the notorious foe of John in the infamous encounter at the baths of Ephesus.[151] To both Cerinthus and the Ebionites, Christ entered the man Jesus at his baptism and left Him just before His passion. While Jesus suffered, the Christ remained untouched by suffering as an angelic being. This Christology is, of course, intolerable to the writer of Hebrews (Hebrews 4:15).

In his epistle to the Galatians, Paul discusses how these churches are observing "special days, months, seasons and years (Galatians 4:10)" which is most certainly reflecting the judaizing controversy. Paul here is speaking in the manner of Isaiah the prophet (1:14), who spoke for God saying "your New Moon festivals and your appointed feasts my soul hates." Why? Concerns for these matters and failure to practice justice and mercy (v. 17) reflect a misplaced priority then and now. Paul reflects the spirit of the prophet as does James, his supposed counter-weight in Jerusalem, who said in his epistle: "If you really keep the royal law found in Scripture, 'Love your neighbor as yourself' (Leviticus 19:18; Matthew 22:39) you are doing right (James 2:8)."

At Qumran, concern over "special days," or calendar, is reflected in several documents. The Dead Sea Scroll writers appear to have missed the point of Isaiah 1:14, though they seem to have a deep seated reverence for Isaiah. They appear to put more weight on when to designate times for festivals and celebrations, but ignore Isaiah's concerns for mercy.

According to Eisenman and Wise, there were several calendars available to Jews during the Second Temple period. The preferred calendar used at Qumran was solar, based on 364 days. This was not the preferred calendar elsewhere in Israel.[152] According to Eisenman and Wise, the advantage of the solar calendar used by the Qumran community, as opposed to the lunar-solar calendar of 354 days used by the Pharisees (and later adopted by Rabbinic Judaism), was that with a solar calendar, holy days, Sabbaths, and festivals would be fixed. There were a significant number of texts that dealt with calendar issues (4Q317, 4Q 318, 4Q320, 4Q321, and 4Q327), and other texts that deal with them in part. This suggests that the calendar was very important in governing the affairs of the community. This concern for the proper calendar is also indicative that the community was largely made up of disaffected lesser priests. Central for these priests, was the priestly rotation described in 1 Chronicles 24:6-19, a part of the priestly duties (*mišmeret*) associated first with the tabernacle, and later with the Temple service.[153]

The priestly rotation would occur weekly and the service of each group would be required every six years. Thus, there was a need within the Qumran community to reconcile the calendars because the lunar calendar of 354 days used in Jerusalem would fall behind the solar calendar of 364 days ten days every year. Every three years the lunar calendar would be attenuated by an additional month of thirty days. This attenuation would fit nicely in the six year cycle. The original rotation is laid out for us in 1 Chronicles 24:7-18 and begins in Jehoiarib (Joiarib in the Qumran texts). In the Qumran texts, however, the rotation begins in Nisan (March-April) because of an understanding that the Creation took place in the spring.[154]

4Q317 is a short fragment that records the phases of the moon throughout the month. One can only guess what this information was used for. Other fragments, described as follows, make it clear that the Qumran community had practitioners of astrology and divination and that this practice was at least tolerated.

4Q318, also called the Brontologion, is a text that resorts to divination to predict the future based on observations as to where thunder can be heard in the skies (hence the name 'brontologion,' the Greek word *brontos*, which means "thunder").

> This Qumran text records the movements of the moon with respect to the signs of the zodiac and combines that approach with the hearing of thunder. Thus the scheme stipulates that if the moon is in a certain sign of the zodiac (and it will be in that sign several times during the year) when one hears thunder, then a certain event of importance to the entire nation will happen.[155]

This resorting to divination and astrology is startling because it appears to be forbidden in the Law of God (Deuteronomy 18:10, 14). In fact, a reason cited for putting to death Balaam, son of Beor, was that he practiced divination (*qāsam*).[156] However, it is clear that divination, though prohibited, was commonly practiced by the peoples of the fertile crescent at the time of Abraham and apparently continued in popularity to the period of the writing of the Qumran documents. Indicative of the widespread acceptance of divination in the ancient world, Jewish Palestine included, even Josephus tells us that the seven branches of the menorah symbolized the seven planets (there were seven known planets at this time, counting the sun and the moon) and the twelve loaves of showbread.[157]

According to Eisenman and Wise, 4Q320 presents the first three years of an attempt to bring some sort of correspondence between the lunar-solar calendar used at the Temple and the strictly solar calendar used at Qumran. An extra month would be inserted at the end of the three-year period because the lunar-solar calendar loses ten days per year, as previously indicated.[158]

4Q321 is particularly interesting because it appears to be an attempt to reconcile the solar calendar used at Qumran with the lunar-solar one used at the Temple in Jerusalem. This document contains some astronomical information. Presumably, the astronomical calculations were performed to verify the accuracy of the lunar reckoning.

4Q327 is a two-fragment document that preserves in part a calendar that highlights the days on which Sabbaths fall. Of course, Sabbath observance is extremely important for all Jews because it is the Fourth Commandment (Exodus 20). Perhaps this highlighting of Sabbaths would be useful to those moving between two calendar systems, the lunar-solar of the Temple and the solar of Qumran.

It is my belief that Paul knew of this dispute over calendars "new moons" (lunar) and "Sabbaths" and saw it creeping into the church as a result of the judaizing influence. The judaizers themselves, coming from a community preoccupied with calendars used for purposes of divination as well as for disputations over Sabbath observance, would seek to confuse Paul's converts with these distractions. Therefore, it is not surprising that these practices were attacked by Paul.

CHAPTER TEN: God's Unfailing Love— 'Ḥesed' in the Old Testament and the Dead Sea Scrolls and its Relation to the Grace of God in the New Testament

The segolete *ḥesed,* translated as "unfailing love" in the New International Version, refers to faithfulness and mercy—first, between men and second, between God and His people. The stories of *ḥesed* in the Bible also point out men's successes and failures in reciprocity. In both the Old Testament and in the Dead Sea Scrolls, *ḥesed* along with its cognates has taken on an integral role of helping us understand the grace of God, as revealed in Christ in the New Testament.

First of all, it is necessary to clear up some confusion as to what the word really means as applied to transactions both between men and between God and man. In 1927, Nelson Glueck wrote a dissertation in German, later translated by Alfred Gottschalk, on the meaning of *ḥesed.*[159] In his dissertation, Glueck contradicted the accepted understanding of the meaning of the word which was "love, kindness, mercy"[160] and insisted that the word really meant "covenant obligation." This would imply that there was a bond of obligation between men, but not motivated necessarily out of love. Also, this was the same between men and God: Israel would be rewarded with military victories as they were obedient. The word was seen to mean "loyalty to covenant obligation" rather than "mercy." However, the best way to understand the meaning of a word is to see how it is used in a given context. I feel that a reading through of the usage of *ḥesed* in the Old Testament does supports Glueck's contention of a reciprocity of obligation, but that its meaning implies much more. In the Dead Sea Scrolls the obligatory nature of *ḥesed* is more apparent.

Ḥesed as Exercised Between Man and Man in the Old Testament

Genesis 20:13; 21:23. In this passage, Abraham and Sarah had moved into the region of the Negev between Kadesh and Shur which was administered by Abimelech, King of Gerar. Abraham was afraid and thought Abimelech would have him killed and take Sarah from him. So, as an act of self-preservation Abraham told Sarah to prove her love (*ḥesed*) to him: she would tell Abimelech that she was Abraham's sister. Abraham was asking Sarah to show him loyalty based upon an already established covenant of marriage. This action on the part of Abraham caused a problem for Abimelech. He had a dream and in the dream he found out that Sarah was really Abraham's wife. Abimelech, then, released Sarah back to Abraham and also gave him sheep, cattle and slaves. Abimelech recognized that God was with Abraham and made a treaty with him. Abimelech asked Abraham to extend to him and his descendents the same kindness (*hesed*) that he had extended to Abraham, and Abraham agreed.

Joshua 2:12,13. Joshua and the Children of Israel were about to cross Jordan and attack Jericho. Two spies were sent beforehand and were hidden by Rahab, a harlot in the city of Jericho. She requested that when the spies were to return to their camp, that they show her and her family kindness (*hesed*) because she had saved their lives. There was apparently no motivation for Rahab to save the spies other than that she had heard about the exploits of the God of Israel (2:9-11) and saw that the Israelites would be favored in the upcoming battle. Her original loyalty was to the king of the city, but the news of God drying up the water of the Red Sea and the destruction of the kingdoms of Og and Shihon was apparently enough to convince her to switch sides. She later became an ancestor of both David (Ruth 4:22) and Jesus (Matthew 1:5; Luke 3:31).

Judges 1:24. When the two tribes from Joseph went to attack Luz (later renamed Bethel) they sent two spies who confronted a man of the city saying, "show us how to get into the city and we will see that you are treated well (*hesed*)." He did, and when the city fell under the ban (see note 31, Chapter One, "was put to the sword") he and his whole family were spared in similar fashion as Rahab. Just like Rahab, this unnamed man had no motivation to help the spies except that he apparently believed they would be victorious. He probably heard the same stories as Rahab in Jericho. Unlike Rahab, he didn't stay with the Israelites, but went and built another Luz in the land of the Hittites.

Ruth 1:8, 2:20, 3:10. Ruth is a very important little book because it tells the story of the kinsman-redeemer (*gōēl*)[161] who saved Naomi and Ruth from destitution and provided the ancestor of Israel's greatest king— David. In this culture, it was very important to keep land ownership within a family (Genesis 38:8; Leviticus 25:25; Deuteronomy 25:5, 6); because that was the way one earned a living. If a landowner died without an heir, then the next of kin had the responsibility to acquire the land and everything belonging to that owner-- including livestock and wives. The first son born to the wife he acquired was given the name of the dead relative and this first-born son inherited the property. By doing this, the widow of the deceased was provided for and the family name and ownership of the land and property continued.

What is remarkable in this story is a series of unprovoked kindnesses (ḥesed): First, Naomi acknowledges that Ruth and Orpah had already shown kindness (ḥesed) to her when they stayed with her after their husbands' deaths. Orpah then leaves, but Ruth continues to stay with Naomi even though she was young enough to find another husband in Moab. She may have acted out of loyalty, but it was not required, as was made clear when her sister left. By staying with Naomi, she could help her out financially (Ruth 1:8-22).

Second, Naomi acknowledges the kindness (ḥesed) of Boaz, a kinsman-redeemer, who had allowed Ruth to glean from his field. It is not entirely clear if he did this out of loyalty as a kinsman-redeemer or if he just found Ruth to be attractive—maybe both. Last, Boaz acknowledges Ruth's kindness (ḥesed) to him because she wants him to marry her and does not want to run after younger men. In all of these instances of ḥesed, loyalty was involved in some way, but was not obligated.

<u>1 Samuel 15:6.</u> This passage is very interesting because it tells us that Saul, on the way to ambush and destroy the Amalekites, warned the Kenites to separate themselves from the Amalekites to save themselves because they "showed kindness (ḥesed) to all the Israelites when they came up out of Egypt." Before this passage, the only other references to the Kenites are Genesis 15:19, Numbers 24:21, 22 and Judges 4:11. The Genesis passage tells us that the Kenites lived in the land that the Israelites would eventually conquer.

Numbers 24:21, 22 is a portion of the fourth oracle given to Balaam in which was said that "the dwelling place [of the Kenites] is secure" though they would eventually be destroyed by Asshur (the Assyrians in the Eighth century B.C.E.). However, we still don't know what they did or would do to earn the favor of the Israelites. In Judges 4:11 we have an indication as to how they earned favor. During the Israelite attack upon Sisera's army, Sisera fled the Israelites to the tent of Jael, Heber the Kenite's wife. Jael killed Sisera while he was napping by driving a tent peg through his head, thus fulfilling Deborah's prophecy that God would hand Sisera over to a woman (Judges 4:9). This indicates the far-reaching effects of ḥesed, because apparently out of loyalty to the memory of this single event, a

kindness was extended to the entire Kenite clan. Yet there was no indication that this loyalty was required contractually.

1 Samuel 20:8, 14, 15; 2 Samuel 9:1, 3, 7. This is a wonderful story of friendship between Jonathan, son of Saul, and David, the future king. David meets up with Jonathan, the king's son and his friend, and asks why his father Saul is trying to kill him. Jonathan denies this could be true until David swears an oath, forming a covenant (*brît*) with Jonathan, that it is true. Because of the covenant, David asks Jonathan to show kindness (*hesed*) if true and death if false. Jonathan knows that David will eventually become king and asks David to show kindness (*hesed*) to him and his family in turn and make a covenant with him. David, in turn, renews his oath (v. 14-17). It is clear that the starting point for the covenant was an already present, deep and abiding friendship between the two young men. The evocation of covenant and *hesed* was to confirm an extension of that friendship across generations and through any future circumstance.

The story picks up again in 2 Samuel 9 when David, after the deaths of Saul and Jonathan, inquires if there are any members of the House of Saul left to whom he may show kindness (*hesed*). When Mephibosheth, son of Jonathan, is brought to him, David tells him not to be afraid because he will honor the covenant he made with his father and will show him kindness (*hesed*). Mephibosheth ends up eating at the king's table. However, the covenant may have been revoked when Mephibosheth turned on him during the revolt of Absalom (2 Samuel 16:3-4).

2 Samuel 2:5; 3:8. In the first instance, *hesed* is used to describe the action of the men of Jabesh Gilead in burying their former king, Saul. Though they might have been inclined not to do so because of Saul's rash and reckless reign, they honored the office of the king and that is what provoked David to praise them. In the second instance, Abner, who was a commanding officer in the army of Saul, was angered when Ishbosheath, one of Saul's surviving sons, accused him of taking one of Saul's concubines. Abner makes it clear that he is still loyal (*hesed*) to the House of Saul. In other words, he could kill Ishbosheath if he wanted to, but did not out of loyalty to Saul.

2 Samuel 10:2; 1 Chronicles 19:2. There is no record of Nahash the Ammonite helping David. In fact, in 1 Samuel 11 we have a record of

Nahash besieging Jabesh Gilead and threatening to make these people his slaves. Fortunately for them, Saul mustered troops to defeat the Ammonites and saved the people of Jabesh Gilead. Perhaps Nahash, being an enemy of Saul, had become a friend of David while David was fleeing from Saul. If Nahash showed kindness (ḥesed) to David, then David would want to return the favor to Nahash's son, Hanun, following the death of Nahash.

2 Samuel 16:17. When Absalom rebelled against his father David, he was surprised to see Hushai, David's friend, greeting him in Jerusalem as king. He said to Hushai, "Is this the love (ḥesed) you show your friend?" Little did he know that he was not disloyal to David as it appeared, but was planning to counsel Absalom wrongly so that Absalom would be defeated and David would return to the throne.

1 Kings 2:7. On his deathbed, David makes a request to his son Solomon to extend kindness (ḥesed) to the family of Barzillai because he had stood with David during the revolt of Absalom. Perhaps Solomon's reign would not be possible without the action of Barzillai, and David wants this acknowledged.

2 Chronicles 24:22. In Chapter 22-23, Jehoiada the priest, in loyalty to the House of David, hid Joash, the future king, from Ahaziah--a powerful woman determined to destroy the remaining potential heirs. By doing this, he was showing kindness (ḥesed) to Joash and the House of David. However, when Joash became king he had Zechariah, son of Jehoiada, killed because Zechariah dared to criticize the king for turning to idols. This breach in ḥesed caused Zechariah in his dying breath to say, "May the Lord see this and call you to account."

Esther 2:9, 17. It is clear that Esther pleased the king of Persia, for she found favor (ḥesed) in his sight. The use of the word ḥesed indicates the king's loyalty to Esther, a loyalty that would eventually come to her favor when Haman tried to destroy all the Jews living in the Persian Empire. It was probably on the basis of this loyalty that king Xerxes agreed to hear the unprecedented request of Esther on behalf of the Jews (Esther 5).

A common thread running through all of these passages is loyalty. What motivates that loyalty differs. Sometimes it is based upon a prior action, and a covenant is either assumed or actual as in the story of Abraham,

Sarah and Abimelech, the story of Saul and the Kenites, the story of David and Nahash, the story of Solomon and Barzillai, and the story of Joash and Jehoiada. At other times, though, this loyalty appears to be founded on a desire of the heart—initiated by the perpetrator and accepted by the object of affection as in the story of Ruth, in the story of David and Jonathan, in the story of Esther, and possibly in the story of the men of Jabesh Gilead who buried the body of Saul. In some instances, loyalty comes when it is clear that self-preservation necessitates it, as in the story of Rahab and the spies.

ḥesed Between God and Man in the Old Testament

Genesis 24: 12, 14, 49; Micah 7:20. This story has Abraham sending his servant back to Abraham's homeland to find a wife for his son Isaac from among his relatives. Before the servant goes, Abraham has him take a solemn oath (24:2-4)[162] not to bring back a wife from among the Canaanites. When he arrives at his destination in Nahor, he prays and asks God to show kindness (ḥesed), that is, loyalty to his covenant promise that he made to Abraham in Genesis 15:5 to make his offspring as the stars in the sky. Genesis 24:49 extends this covenant to include the actions of Abraham's relatives Laban and Bethuel. Abraham had offered to have these people in Nahor as part of the fulfillment of God's declaration that he would be "father of multitudes." Micah 7:20 affirms that God will fulfill His purposes by showing mercy (ḥesed) to Abraham and his descendents according to his own pledged fidelity.

Genesis 39:21. The Lord was working his plan through Joseph and therefore showed him kindness (ḥesed) by helping him gain favor with the prison warden. Joseph had a role in God's plan for preserving the children of Israel through a famine in the region. Part of the that plan was to set in motion a series of events that would propel Joseph into a position of responsibility in Egypt that would ultimately benefit the children of Israel and God's plan for blessing the world through Joseph's people. This is more than just a simple act of kindness to Joseph. It is a declaration of God's sovereignty in the scheme of things.

Exodus 20:6, 34:6; Numbers 14:18; Deuteronomy 5:10; Psalm 103:8; 145:8; Jeremiah 32:18; Joel 2:13; Jonah 4:2. All of these passages have in common the statement that God is "showing love" or "abounding in love (ḥesed)" to generations that follow. As in the story of Joseph, God is declaring his sovereignty over this world: His purposes will not be frustrated. In Exodus 20:6 the comparison is made between the fact that sin brings consequences to the generations that follow, but that God limits these to only three or four generations. In contrast, God extends love or kindness to a thousand generations because of the action of obedience by one. Christians believe that the most obvious example of kindness extended to "a thousand generations" through the obedience of one man is Jesus, called Christ whose action of obedience culminating in His death on the cross affects positively the lives of multitudes of people today.

2 Samuel 22:51; Psalm 18:50. Once again, God's sovereignty is proclaimed in his dealings with the children of Israel, or in this case with the house of David particularly. God shows unfailing kindness (*ḥesed*) to David and his descendents not in randomness on the one hand, nor out of obligation on the other. Christians believe that God shows this kindness and favor because it works to further his interests in ultimately bringing his Son into the world. David had little inclination toward understanding just how prophetic he was when he declared God's unfailing love was upon his anointed (*māšîāḥ*), the descendents of David forever.

Ezra 9:9. At first, Ezra acknowledges the sins of his people that had sent Israel into captivity for the past seventy years. Then, he also acknowledges that despite these sins, God has shown kindness (*ḥesed*) to his people by granting them favor in the eyes of the king of Persia and granting them the privilege of rebuilding the Temple and wall around Jerusalem. This also is a declaration of God's sovereignty and the part His kindness has in God's plan. God is not through with His people.

Psalm 25:10; 32:10; 33:5; 51:1; 61:7; 86:5; 89:2, 14; 101:1; Psalm 103:4, 8; Micah 7:18. Psalms 25:10, 32:10 and 86:5 appear to put conditions on God's love (*ḥesed*)—one must be in covenant with Him and trust in Him to receive His love. However, it may be better to understand that being in covenant and actively trusting God puts oneself in a position to receive God's love much as being alongside a raging stream puts one in a position of partaking of its refreshing water. Psalms 33:5; 51:1; 89:2, 14; Psalm 101:1, Psalm103:4 and Micah 7:18 simply speak of God's love (*ḥesed*) in more or less general terms. God's love is associated with His faithfulness and is a part of His nature.

<u>Psalm 57:3; 85:10-11; Jeremiah 9:24</u>. In God, all qualities such as love (*ḥesed*), faithfulness, righteousness and peace come together. To define these qualities, the starting point must be God.

<u>Jeremiah 2:2; Hosea 4:1; 6:6; 10:12; 12:6; Micah 6:8</u>. These passages chide God's people for their lack of *ḥesed* toward God. God is faithful to His covenant, but His people are not. This is true even in Hosea 6:6 and Micah 6:8, where *ḥesed* is translated "mercy" in the NIV. Of course, God wants us to be kind and merciful to each other, but primarily God wants us to show kindness and mercy toward Him!

<u>Jeremiah 31:3</u>. God reminds His people through the testimony of past events that His love (*ḥesed*) was always the motivating factor in His dealings with His people. Therefore, by implication God will continue to show His mercy not based on their faithfulness. In fact, He will use love (*ḥesed*) to draw them out of unfaithfulness.

In looking at all of these passages describing God's dealings with His people we note that God is faithful or loyal to the benefit of His people even though they might be unfaithful towards Him. This loyalty springs not from a sense of randomness or obligation, but from faithfulness to covenant (*brît*). In fact, in virtually all relationships between men in Semitic culture and between men and God, an implicit or explicit sense of *brît* is present.[163]

What is *brît* in the Old Testament? Eichrodt makes a wonderful statement about the religious *brît*:

> The covenant knows not only of a demand, but also of a promise: 'You shall be my people and I will be your God.' In this way it provides life with a goal and history with a meaning. Because of this the fear that constantly haunts the pagan world, the fear of arbitrariness and caprice in the Godhead, is excluded. With this God men know exactly where they stand; *an atmosphere of trust and security* [italics are Eichrodt's] is created, in which they find both the strength for a willing surrender to the will of God and joyful courage to grapple with the problems of life.[164]

God makes a covenant with Abraham and his descendents, then more specifically with David and his descendants, and then with *ḥesed* demonstrates his unswerving faithfulness, not according to the merits of these people, but according to His own character: He is faithful to His covenant.

Ḥesed in the Dead Sea Scrolls

The word *ḥesed* appears frequently in the Dead Sea Scrolls. In CD, the *Manual of Discipline* and in the *War Scroll* the word comes with enough context to determine its meaning. *ḥesed* also appears in a number of other fragments, but for the most part, the context cannot be discerned.

The Damascus Document (CD)

In CD 13, the *mĕbaqqēr* or Bishop of the community (see Chapter One) is the one responsible for instruction and has the authority to examine novices. Nothing may be done without his approval. The members of the community also have ranking authority (13:12). Consequently, in 13:18 the community is exhorted to reprove a member in a compromising situation (divorce?) with compassionate love (*ḥesed*). Both the discipline and response revolve around the concept of loyalty with which each member is bound to the other.

The word *ḥesed* appears again in CD 20:21, but this time reference is made to Exodus 20:6, which explains that the love of God extends to thousands because of the faithfulness of one. Still, the initial love of God is dependent on the faithfulness of the one in the context of obedience to God's law.

Manual of Discipline

In the *Manual of Discipline*, the community is often referred to as "the community of kindness (*ḥesed*) or compassionate love (1QS 1:8; 2:24; 5:4, 25; 10:26)." The community is self-conscious about its role in God's covenant and takes its obligation toward loyalty quite seriously. In 1QS 8:2, the community seeks to imitate God as exemplified in Psalm 85:10 and Jeremiah 9:24 in the way it conducts its business. They see themselves as the remnant of Israel.

In 1QM 14:4 and the parallel passage in another version of the War Scroll (4Q491 f8_10i:2), God is viewed as the one who remains merciful because of His loyalty to his covenant. The people of God (the remnant at Qumran) are redeemed and therefore are following the conditions of the covenant (e.g. works of *tôrā*—see Chapter Two). God is under covenant obligation to deliver them.

Hymns (1QH[a])

The *Hodayoth* (1QH[a] 4:18; 8:17, 24-25; 15:20; 19:17; 20:14) are celebratory of the fact that God has drawn the community members into covenant and have, therefore, become the objects of God's compassion (*ḥesed*) or favor. In 13:22 the community itself is referred to as the poor (*ᶜānāvîm* see Chapter One) of compassion (*ḥesed*). Though they are in a state of poverty, they never cease being objects of God's mercy and they, in turn, return that love to God.

As in the Old Testament, the common thread running through the use of *ḥesed* is loyalty. God establishes a covenant with his people and remains faithful to those who respond in kind. It is understood that God's people have trouble remaining faithful to Him, but God is merciful if they repent. In many ways this understanding of God's dealing with His people presupposes the New Testament. However, this compassion seems to be mainly vertical. Though compassion is applied between members of the community, this compassion appears to be obligatory and not voluntary. The members are loyal to one another because they are bound to each other in the same covenant relationship to God.

Ḥesed is usually translated *eleos* in the LXX which can be translated in turn as "mercy," "compassion" or "pity." *Eleos* is used in Genesis 24:12, 14, and 49; Exodus 20:6 and 34:7; Ruth 1:8; 1 Samuel 15:6, 20:14; 18, 2 Samuel 9:1, 3, 7; 2 Samuel 3:8, 22:51; 1 Kings 2:7; Ezra 9:9; Psalm 18:50; 25:10; 32:10; 33:5; 61:7; 89:2, 14; 101:1, 103:4; Jeremiah 9:24; Hosea 4:1; 6:6; 12:6; Micah 6:8; 7:18. *ḥesed* is translated *charis* ("grace") in Genesis 39:21, *eleēmōn* ("merciful") in Exodus 34:6; Psalm 103:8, *polueleos* ("very merciful") in Numbers 14:18, *chrēstos* ("kind," "loving") in Psalm 86:5, *oiktirēma* ("mercy," "compassion") in Jeremiah 31:3, *dikaiosunē* in Hosea 10:12 ("righteousness").

In transactions between men such as expressed in 1 Samuel 20 and 2 Chronicles 24:22, a breach of *hesed* carries significant legal implications ("may the Lord deal with me ever so severely" and "may the Lord see this and call you to account"). Contracts with *hesed* may or may not begin with emotional love and compassion, but they are primarily legal contracts with expected loyalty enforced by legal or social sanctions. However, most of the Greek words used to translate *hesed* (with the possible exception of *dikaiosunē*) are more emotive than the original Hebrew word may have been.[165] What is particularly interesting here is that the LXX translators used words that emphasized the feelings of love without the presumed loyalty enforced by law or cultural expectation. For them, perhaps, the emotive was the focus and by this conscious or unconscious (one cannot know for sure) choice of words, Greek readers of the Old Testament might miss more of the broader implications of *hesed*. This would pave the way for a more compassionate and a less cold contractual understanding of God and the community of the faithful in the time of Jesus.

The Cognates *ḥassîdîm* (*ḥāssîdê, ḥāssîd*)

In the Dead Sea Scrolls, *ḥassîdîm* is found in 4Q521 (f2ii 4:5, 7) and in the apocryphal psalm text 11Q5 (11QPs[a]) 18:10, 22:3. It is also found in the biblical Psalms 149 (1, 5), but scripture portions containing these verses have not been found at Qumran or at nearby finds of scrolls from the period. In Psalm 149:1, 5 *ḥassîdîm* can be translated "the sanctified" and appears to be speaking about all of Israel. *ḥāssîdê* is not found in the non-biblical Qumran literature, but is found in Psalm 50:5 where it means ones sanctified or "pious ones" gathered before God "to cut a covenant by sacrifice" referring, perhaps, to the administrators of the sacrificial system (priests) in the Temple. Psalm 50:5 is also in the 11Q9 (11QPs[e]) Qumran text. In the LXX the word is translated as *hosios* or "holy ones."

ḥāssîd is also not found in the non-biblical documents at Qumran, but is found in 2 Sam. 22:26; Psalms 4:4; 12:2; 18:26; 32:6; 43:1; 86:2; Jeremiah 3:12; and Micah 7:2 where it can be translated as "godly" or "righteous." In the LXX, the word is translated as *hosios*, except in Jeremiah and Micah where it is translated with *eleēmōn* and *eulabēs* respectively. The Jeremiah passage has *ḥāssîd* applied to God rather than man, and so *eleēmōn* meaning "merciful" is used. *Eulabēs* can be translated "devout" or "reverent."

'Eleos' in the New Testament

A study of *eleos* (or the verb form *eleeō*) in the New Testament needs a more extensive treatment than is possible here, but by a cursory look at how it is used in the gospels and letters of Peter and Paul, enough can be discerned. In the synoptic gospels, except for Matthew 5:7 where *eleos* means "merciful" in the Sermon on the Mount and Luke 16:24 where Abraham is asked to help in Jesus' parable of the Rich man and Lazarus, the word is used in an address to Jesus: "Lord, son of David have mercy on me" (Matthew 15:22); "Lord, have mercy on my son" (Matthew 17:15), "Have mercy on us, Son of David (Matthew 9:27; Matthew 20:30; Mark 10:47; Luke 18:38, 39), "Jesus, Master have pity (mercy) on us" (Luke 17:13). In these passages, *eleos* is used as part of an appeal to Jesus' compassion in his role as Messiah and Son of God. Perhaps this is indicative of the recognition among Jesus' followers as well as other Jews of the Second Temple period (see Chapters Four and Five) of the eternal nature of the Messiah and his reign.

Throughout the New Testament *eleos* continues to play its part in God's dealings with man and with the actions of men with men in the community of faith. Romans 11:30-32 points up the sovereignty of God in conferring *eleos* upon Gentiles who were once disobedient at the expense of Israel, who is now the disobedient. In Romans 12:8 Paul encourages *eleos* in the community of believers. In 1 Corinthians 7:25, 2 Corinthians 4:1, Philippians 2:27, 1 Timothy 1:13 and 16 *eleos* continues to be used positively to highlight God's sovereignty. In 2 Timothy, Paul attaches great significance to *eleos* when he puts it, along with "grace" and "peace," in his opening greetings (2:2).

In 2 Timothy 1:15-18, Paul prays that God would grant *eleos* to the family of Onesiphorus because, from loyalty, he had greatly benefited Paul. James proclaims the sovereignty of *eleos* over judgment (James 2:13), and speaks of *eleos* as a characteristic of the "wisdom that comes from heaven (James 3:17)." In 1 Peter 2:10, Peter echoes Paul's understanding of mercy as expressed in Romans 11. By linking *eleos* with God's sovereign will, the Old Testament understanding of *ḥesed* is approached. Still, the compassionate element intrinsic to *eleos* is thrust in the forefront.

In conclusion, we comprehend a world of implications behind the word *eleos* as used in the New Testament. For if we understand the nature of *ḥesed*, that its primary meaning is "covenant loyalty," then when we come to the use of *eleos* it is fair to assume the same expectations for relationships between both man and God on the one hand, and men with men on the other.

We know that as Christians we have an obligation to fulfill the law of love as exemplified by Jesus himself, "love the Lord your God with all your heart, with all your soul, and with all your mind" (that is with every fiber of our being), and "love your neighbor as yourself (Matthew 22:37-40)." Practically speaking, this means that we are loyal first to God and then to our bothers and sisters in Christ. When the whole community practices *ḥesed/eleos* then that same community can, in the words of Eichrodt mentioned earlier, stand in "an atmosphere of trust and security" both with one another and with God.

CHAPTER ELEVEN: Issues of Authority and Hermeneutics— Interpretation of the Old Testament at Qumran and in the New Testament Community

Before we can actually discuss Qumran and early New Testament community hermeneutics, we must understand what was considered authoritative to each community and if and in what way this consideration differed from contemporaries in the Second Temple period. For, if a work is not considered authoritative then it would most likely be handled differently. First, we will examine the rabbinic approach, then the approach that Jesus and the apostles took in identifying authoritative scripture. Then we will compare the Qumran and New Testament hermeneutic.

Rabbinic Authority

According to F. F. Bruce, the Qumran commentators, the Pharisees (rabbinic tradition) and the Sadducees were in substantial agreement as to the limits of Hebrew Scripture.[166] All agreed that the authoritative books were the ones essentially "canonized" during Ezra's reforms in 458 B.C.E. The Rabbis, and more particularly the school of Hillel[167] recognized a three-part arrangement discussed during the period between the first (70 C.E.) and second (132 C.E.) Jewish wars against the Romans and recorded as a *baraitha* in the *Baba Bathra* tractate of the Babylonian Talmud.[168] Following the destruction of the Temple in 70 C.E. at the so-called council of Jamnia, the Rabbis discussed and *recognized as already authoritative* the books we presently have as part of the Protestant and Jewish Old Testament canon.

Apostolic Authority

In the New Testament, Jesus and the apostles were clear on how they arrived at what *they* regarded as authoritative.[169] Even though we cannot be certain whether or not the same set of books regarded today as canonical and authoritative were the same as that in the first century, there is evidence that Jesus recognized the same three-fold division of authoritative scripture as the Rabbis: the arrangement began with Genesis and ended with 2 Chronicles.[170] In Luke 11:50f and Matthew 23:35, Jesus refers to the blood of the prophets from Abel (Genesis) to Zechariah son of Jehoiada (2 Chronicles 24:20-22).[171]

Christians look at Jesus' approach to Scripture, and then the way the apostle's approached Scripture as standard in identifying first what is authoritative, then in developing a hermeneutic for that authority. Jesus and the apostles would often, but not exclusively, use a form of "it is written" to precede a quote from what they determined to be Scripture. As it turns out, Jesus and the apostles used this approach to quote from many of the books of the Old Testament that Protestants and Jews regard today as authoritative, but would not use this approach to quote from non-authoritative writings.

Jesus in Matthew 4:4-10 (Luke 4:4-10) quotes from Deuteronomy and the Psalms as authoritative, and again quotes from Zechariah as authoritative in Matthew 26:31. Peter quotes from the Psalms in this manner in Acts 1:20, James in Acts 15:15 quotes from Amos 9 in this manner, and in Acts 23:5 Paul quotes from Exodus 22 following this same pattern. Paul uses the phrase to refer to Habakkuk 2 in Romans 1:17, Isaiah and Ezekiel in Romans 2:24, Psalms, Ecclesiastes and again Isaiah in Romans 3, and Genesis in Romans 4:17. Other Old Testament books of the present canon referred to in the New Testament in this manner are Malachi, 1 Kings, Jeremiah, 2 Samuel, and Leviticus.[172]

Another way Jesus and the apostles would point out what was authoritative was to refer to a document as "scripture" (in LXX, Daniel 9:2 *tais biblois* with reference to Jeremiah, or *ba sēperim* "by means of the Scriptures" canonical books;[173] in the New Testament *tais graphais* or [*ta*] *hiera grammata* "the writings/the holy Scriptures"). It is interesting that Peter in 2 Peter 3:16 refers to Paul's letters as Scripture on par with "the other Scriptures" (*tas loipas graphas*) or the Old Testament. Jesus used this terminology to identify Psalms in Matthew 21:42, and Exodus in Matthew 22:29, as authoritative. Paul in Romans 15:3, 4 identified the phrase "it is written" with Psalm 69:6, calling it Scripture. James referenced Leviticus as "scripture" (*graphēn*) in James 2:8.

The apostles and even Jesus might refer to some writings found at Qumran that were later regarded as non-canonical (for example, Tobit in Matthew 7:12 and Luke 6:31[174] and Enoch in Jude 14) without referencing them as "Scripture," or employing the designation "it is written." Sometimes the

New Testament writers would refer, in a non-authoritative manner, to documents of which we do not have an extant copy (*"The Assumption of Moses"* allegedly quoted by Jude in v. 9).[175]

The Text

The difference between the Old Testament of the Rabbinic tradition, which later developed into what we know today as the Masoretic text, and that of the early church is not in the books which were regarded as authoritative, but in the *text*. We know that from the time of Stephan's defense in Acts 7 that the church made extensive use of the LXX as their translation (c. 200 B.C.E.) of the Holy Scriptures into Greek. There can be no doubt, for example, that the biblical quotations used by Stephan as presented by the narrator Luke were, for the most part, taken from the LXX.[176] When Paul argued before the Thessalonians in Acts 17, his biblical support came via the LXX, and it was from the LXX that Paul got biblical support when he argued at the Aeropagus in Athens in Acts 17.[177]

This Greek text was based on an earlier Hebrew textual family arising in Palestine, whereas the Masoretic text (900 C.E.) was based on a proto-Rabbinic text from the Babylonian textual family. This is why there is some discrepancy between the protestant and Jewish Old Testament on the one hand and the LXX version on the other hand. For a more complete and excellent discussion on the textual history of the Old Testament, see Frank Moore Cross's article *"The Text behind the Text of the Hebrew Bible"* in **Understanding the Dead Sea Scrolls** mentioned in the notes.

Qumran Authority

Though the Qumran community apparently recognized the same set of books as the Rabbis and Jesus as being authoritative, there were some additional texts found at Qumran (e.g. Tobit, Book of Jubilees, and Book of Enoch), that may have been recognized as Scripture by the community.[178] Later, these books were not considered canonical by the Rabbis or Protestants, but are considered deutro-canonical (with the exception of the Book of Jubilees) by the Roman Catholic Church. In addition, there were some writings present that were evidently not considered authoritative by the Qumran community or anyone that we know of outside that community. The preference for one textual family over another at Qumran is inconclusive. Sometimes, as for example with the books of Chronicles, Jeremiah, and Daniel, the community would have a copy that appears to be from the Babylonian family of texts and others that appear to be Palestinian.[179]   The Second Temple period was obviously a time of some confusion and fluidity regarding authoritative and official texts.

Hartmut Stegemann believes that the Temple Scroll (11Q19 and 11Q20) may itself be a sixth book of *tôrā* composed of Palestinian expansions and additions to the original *tôrā* that were rejected by Ezra, but were, nevertheless, revered by some unknown Jewish group (but not by the Qumran population).[180]   Consistently, many of the *pēšerim* found at Qumran are based upon texts that have more in common with the LXX than with the later Masoretic. For example, in the Habukkuk *pēšer* mentioned in Chapter One (1QpHab 11:13), the text quoted for Habukkuk 2:16 says "Drink up and also stagger!" which agrees with the LXX against the Masoretic which has "Drink and be exposed!"[181]   Interestingly enough, the word "exposed" is better translated "uncircumcised" and though the 1QpHab has "stagger" which seems to fit the context better, the *pēšer* comments as if it means "uncircumcised" (which suggests that both text versions were available to the Qumran commentators)!

How the Qumran Community Interpreted the Bible

As were many of the New Testament writers in their interpretation of biblical texts, Qumran commentators were generally allegorical; they were more concerned with present events and making Scripture conform to their *sitz im leben* than in following any semblance of what modern scholars would call the historical-critical approach to a text.[182]   The use of the *pēšer* or commentary is particularly revealing as to the hermeneutics of the Qumran writers. According to Eisenman and Wise, the "approach usually involved a high degree of esotericism, as the exegesis played on a passage or some vocabulary from older texts…and developed it in the most intense and imaginative manner conceivable, relating it to the present life of the community, its heroes and enemies, and the people of Israel."[183]

The Qumran community also employed the paraphrase as a means of interpretation of biblical texts. Several of these texts were found in cave four (4Q158, 364, 365 also called 4QReworked Pentateuch, 4Q370, 372, 373, 458, 462, and 559) with others found in cave six (6Q19, 20). For example, we can compare a paraphrase of Deuteronomy 5:30 from 4Q158 with the translation of the same passage from a text found in Cave Four (4QDeut) and the NIV:

> And YHWH said to Moses: Go and tell them: Go back to [your tents!].[184]

> ["Go, say to them], 'Return to your tents.'[185]

> "Go, tell them to return to their tents."

It is quite evident that the paraphrase takes a bit of liberty with the text with the addition of the phrase "And YHWH said to Moses" to clarify that it was YHWH who spoke to Moses. The other text from Cave Four is word for word the same as the Masoretic as reflected in the NIV. A reading of other texts from the Reworked Pentateuch and the additional texts mentioned will show similar liberties that make it clear that these are not just variants but deliberate paraphrases of biblical texts.

The Genesis Florilegium

The community did perform rather sophisticated exegesis as evidenced by the Genesis *Pēšer* or 4Q252, a work concerned with reconciling numbers and other apparent discrepancies in Genesis. The author is particularly concerned with the dates of activity in the Flood narrative, probably because of the difference in the use of calendars between the Qumran community, which used a solar calendar, and the Pharisees, who used a lunar calendar (see Chapter Seven).

The solar calendar would give relatively fixed dates, but the lunar calendar would not; the author of the Florilegium felt that this was a particularly vexing problem. Modern textual critics see dating problems in the text and attribute these to a faulty editorial process, probably at the time of Ezra, that brought two different texts called 'P' for priestly, and 'E' for Elohist together to give us the Genesis text. An interesting challenge to this theory has been advanced by William Shea in his article, *"The Structure of the Genesis Flood Narrative and its Implications."*[186]

Another interesting apologetic action concerns the problem of God cursing Canaan instead of his father, Ham. After all, it was Ham who had uncovered his father Noah's nakedness. The author points out that Canaan was cursed because Ham, along with his brothers, had already received a blessing from God (Genesis 9:1), and this blessing could not be removed—not even by God. This interpretation would also confirm the scriptural admonition that one action can affect future generations positively or negatively (Exodus 20:6; Deuteronomy 8:10). The author of the Florilegium is dealing here with a textual problem much as modern defenders of Scripture would handle textual problems.

Eisenman and Wise highlight two points that the author of the Genesis Florilegium was trying to make in columns 4 and 5: (1) the Messiah "of righteousness" (ṣedeq) must come from Judah, so all other rivals, including Saul must be discredited, and (2) sex with a concubine is to be condemned.[187] With reference to the first point, the author takes on the account of Moses' prediction of the destruction of Amalek (Exodus 17:14, Deuteronomy 25:19). In the Genesis account, the Amalekites attacked Israel as they were heading to the Promised Land through Rephidim. As long as Moses held up his hands, Israel would prevail, so Aaron and Hur held up the hands of Moses while Joshua fought Amalek. Moses then promised that in the future Amalek would be utterly wiped out.

The author of the Florilegium *adds* to Moses' prediction the phrase "in the last days"[188] an interpretive note that suggests the importance of this elimination of Amalek for the present (Second Temple period) coming of Messiah. To continue the point being made here, Saul was commissioned by Samuel to be the one to fulfill this prophecy in 1 Samuel 15, but he did not do so. He allowed the king and some sheep to live. Here is the heart of the matter. Saul was rejected as king precisely because he failed to fulfill Moses' prediction—Samuel had to complete the assignment. Therefore, Messiah, who would come "in the last days," could not come from Saul.

The second point, condemnation of sex with a concubine, is brought out with the implication made by the author, that Amalek went bad because he was the product of sex with a concubine. The inherent evil in this relationship is further illustrated by the blessings of Jacob upon his sons (Genesis 49:3-4). Reuben, who is the firstborn and therefore the one who should have gotten the blessing of being the ancestor of Messiah, does not get this honor because he defiled himself with his Father's concubine—Bilhah (Genesis 35:22). This leads to the messianic prophecy of the Scepter which was said over Judah (Genesis 49:10). The prophecy of the Scepter is the prophecy of the rule of Messiah. The whole point of this discussion is that God rejected Saul (and all other lines, i.e., Reuben) and chose David. It is from the Davidic line that Messiah would come.

New Testament Interpretation

We have already pointed out that the Qumran commentators were allegorical in their approach to the Old Testament and that the New Testament writers followed a similar "apocalyptisizing" approach—adapting Old Testament texts to new situations and essentially ignoring their historical situation when they felt justified in doing so. New Testament writers also followed Jewish practice in adapting Old Testament stories to current situations and making use of halakot to interpret the Old Testament. Two examples here illustrate this methodology: Mark 12:1-9 and 1 Corinthians 7:14.

Mark 12:1-9. Recently, Craig Evans began a "dialogue" with J. S. Kloppenborg Verbin over the use of the LXX, MT and Isaiah 5:1-7 in Mark 12:1-9. Evans concludes that, despite Kloppenborg Verbin's intimations to the contrary, Jesus' parable of the Vineyard has definite allusions to the Aramaic influenced paraphrase of Isaiah 5:1-7 and the parable does follow a Semitic hermeneutic orientation in its presentation.[189]

Evans presents his argument with a clarification and three points. First, he makes it clear that the use of the LXX does not prove that Isaiah 5:1-7 was not the backdrop of the original parable. Instead it only proves that the parable passed through hands that sought to standardize Old Testament quotations with the LXX, whether those hands were Mark or the marken redactor. Indeed, as Evans points out as part of his first point, the Mark text agrees with the MT, and I might add the Qumran 1QIsa[a,b,f] texts, against the LXX at points, demonstrating a Hebrew-Aramaic influence on Mark.[190] For example, the 1QIsa texts and MT make use of third person verbs (e.g., "he built) as does Mark, while the LXX uses first person ("I made" and "I dug").

In his second point, Evans demonstrates that Mark 12:1-9 follows the Aramaic paraphrase of Isaiah which must have been familiar to Aramaic speakers reading and interpreting Isaiah in the synagogues of Jesus' time. Both the Aramaic paraphrase and the parable of Mark, which follows the questioning of Jesus' authority by the Temple authorities (11:27-33), have a marked anti-Temple flavor. Allusions to heritage in the Aramaic paraphrase correspond to the parable's "heir" (*klēronomos*) and "inheritance" (*klēronomia*). Also, the Aramaic parable makes more direct reference to the Temple cult in substituting "sanctuary" and "altar" for the MT's "tower" and "winepress." Judgment is the result of a loss of the Shekinah glory of God and places of sanctuary rather then the MT's hedge and wall. Evans final point is that the marken parable follows the themes and elements of rabbinic parables common at the time.

In conclusion, the Jewishness of this parable places the events easily at the time of Jesus. The gospel writer Mark clearly is working with a tradition, oral or otherwise, that is authentic, and one that follows the practices of Jewish storytelling common during the Second Temple period.

1 Corinthians 7:14. The modern interpreter often finds Paul's logic hard to follow in his instruction on marriage and divorce between unbeliever and believer. Some scholars such as Joachim Jeremias and Yonder Gillihan have turned to ancient halakhot with some success in an attempt to understand Paul in this and other passages of Scripture.[191] Gillihan presents an excellent and very comprehensive analysis of the background for Paul's pronouncement on licit marriage and the sanctification of children.

First, both 4QMMT, written in the mid-Second Century B.C.E. (cf. endnote 2) and the Mishnah, compiled around 200 C.E. form the early and latter edges of halakhic activity. Paul's conclusion on licit marriage was composed roughly 55 C.E. which comes right in the middle of this activity. As an observation, it would be unusual if Paul, a self-described Hebrew of the Hebrews (Philippians 3:5) and follower of Jesus who also had made rulings on Jewish law (Chapter One), did *not* make use of halakhot.

Second, both 4QMMT (4Q394-399) and the Mishnah make pronouncements on marriage that can help shed some light on Paul's halakhot. Composite 4QMMT 42-52 pronounces forbidden the joining of those who are impure due to physical defect (discussed in Chapter Three) along with "the Ammonite and the Moabite" and the *mamzerim*, or bastards, which can not be united with an Israelite in marriage, so as to preserve the purity of the temple. The reasoning was that the joining of pure and impure makes both impure as well as their offspring. This endangers the purity of the temple (holy place) and of the people of the land.

In the Mishnah, in the third division under betrothals (*Qiddushin*) the rabbis spoke of the sanctifying effect of marriage. Indeed the words for betrothal and "holiness" or sanctification have the same root (*qdš*). When the rabbis discussed betrothal they assumed the licitness of the union and declared the male Israelite the "sanctifier." In 1 Corinthians 7:14 Paul is using the same language of sanctification. He does not speak of sanctification here as he does elsewhere with reference to a work of the Holy Spirit within an individual who has been justified by faith in Christ, but in a legal sense.

Gillihan points out that the existence of a large Jewish community in Corinth presumes that the church there would be concerned with the status of marriage.[192] Christians may be wondering if their marriage, which may have taken place before one spouse was converted, remains licit if one spouse is unbelieving. Concern also arises as to the status of the children of such a union. Unlike the Qumran writers, Paul focuses on the union after the marriage and pronounces the marriage licit if one spouse is a believer. To do otherwise would make the children unclean, which, in fact, they are not. Unlike the rabbis, Paul makes the believing spouse, not the male, the sanctifier. In addition, he follows the teaching (halakhot) of Jesus who forbids divorce except for infidelity—if the unbelieving spouse would stay in the marriage, the believing spouse should not leave.

Qumran v. New Testament Interpretation of Isaiah 61:1, 2

We have already looked at Isaiah 61:1, 2 and saw that both the Qumran community and the New Testament saw fulfillment of this passage in a messianic figure that would set the world right. The Qumran community believed that this messiah would destroy the foreign Kittîm, whereas the New Testament messiah would have two comings: first, to suffer and die for the sins of the world; second, to judge the world. What is interesting is that each community interpreted this verse according to the situation each found itself in and had little regard as to how Isaiah originally might have understood it.

This passage comes from what many scholars dub "Third Isaiah" (Isaiah 56-66) who follows "Second Isaiah" (Isaiah 40-55). There appears to be a disconnect between Chapters 39 and 40, so these scholars believe a different writer took up pen and ink during the exile and perhaps a disciple of Second Isaiah penned the rest after the return from exile. Most conservative scholars refuse to divide up Isaiah and claim that chapters 40-66 were written prophetically about the exile and its aftermath. Indeed, there is no external evidence that would concur with a division of Isaiah.

Regardless, Isaiah or Third Isaiah was trying to comfort the people of his time either during the siege of Jerusalem by Sennacherib in the eighth century or the people of Jerusalem during the hard times following the return from exile in the sixth century. Isaiah's focus in the section that includes the passage in question begins in Chapter 40. Isaiah seeks to give his people hope in what appears to be a hopeless situation. It is not until the first centuries B.C.E. and C.E. that this passage becomes messianic.

Conclusion

New Testament writers were not at all unique in the *manner* in which they interpreted the Old Testament. The difference between the New Testament writers and their contemporaries was in the substance. New Testament writers made use of apocalyptic imagery, halakhot, paraphrase of scripture, and parables in their efforts to convince others that Jesus is the long-awaited Messiah and the fulfillment of their individual and collective needs and holy desires.

CHAPTER TWELVE: Is 7Q5 a Fragment of the Gospel of Mark?

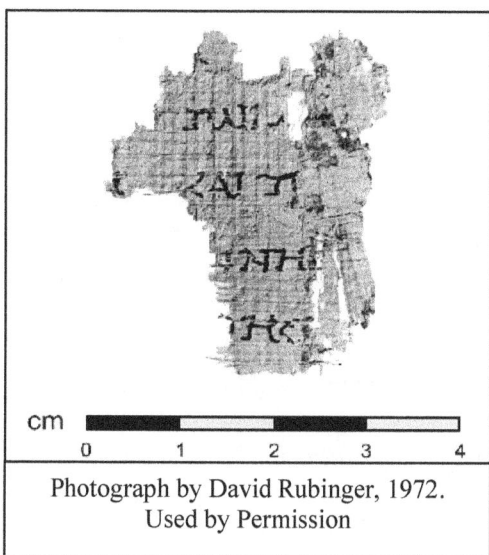

cm
0   1   2   3   4

Photograph by David Rubinger, 1972.
Used by Permission

In 1972, Spanish papyrologist Jose O'Callaghan argued that an obscure Greek fragment found in Qumran Cave Seven is actually a portion of Mark 6:52-53. At least seventeen other distinct Greek papyrus fragments and one imprint of papyrus on hardened clay were discovered in the cave. Two other fragments were deciphered to be Exodus 29:4-7 (7Q1) and the deutero-canonical Letter of Jeremiah 43-44 (7Q2). All others except 7Q5 and one other, which O'Callaghan claimed was a portion of 1 Timothy 3:16 – 4:3, were considered indecipherable. Of the two inscriptions identified by O'Callaghan, only 7Q5 appears to be the most promising.

O'Callaghan based his claim on the positioning of the word *kai* in the third line in relation to the letters *nu nu eta sigma* in the next line. Using the science of stichometry and calculating the average number of letters per line, O'Callaghan found that the letters *nu nu eta sigma* from line four were perfectly in place to be part of the word Gennesaret in Mark 6:53. Understanding that verse 52 was the end of one pericope and verse 53 began another with *kai*, the space in the text before *kai* would be expected. Generally, though, the New Testament scholarly community was not interested.

In 1984, German scholar Carsten Peter Thiede reintroduced O'Callaghan's claims. On April 12, 1992, an enlarged photograph of the fragment investigated by the Division of Identification and Forensic Science of the Investigations Department of the Israeli National Police appeared to buttress O'Callaghan and Thiede's claims for a reading of *autōn* with a trace of a final *nu* in line two. This would be the *autōn* of Mark 6:52.[193] Papyrologist Herbert Hunger has since concurred with O'Callaghan and

Theide that 7Q5 is indeed Markan.[194] Finally, the New Testament scholarly community began to take notice. This *autōn* reading has been discounted by Ernest Muro, Jr. who has contended that the *nu* may actually be an *alpha*. This would agree with R. P. Boismard's original notes to the *editio princeps* [195] of the fragment first published by M. Baillet, J. T. Milik and R. deVaux in 1962.

Contra Thiede, Muro wrote an on-line article first explaining that what Thiede and O'Callaghan believed to be a *nu* in line two was actually an *iota* followed by an *alpha*. He went on to castigate Thiede for his assertion that there is no such alpha appearing in Greek papyri, and cited six examples that appear to contradict Thiede's assertions, calling upon his readers to produce more.[196] From the perspective of this author, the emotional outbursts of both Thiede and Muro are beside the point.

A look at the reconstruction by Moru of an *alpha* in line two by making use of a complete *alpha* in line three does not produce a fit in the eyes of this author. Then, Muro proposed that the right portion of the fragment was actually displaced and suggested line one may contain a *sigma* or an *omega* if the text were realigned. This proposal is admittedly filled with conjecture and this author does not know if others have taken it seriously. Nevertheless, it is another possible (but not necessarily probable) explanation for a non-Markan identification of 7Q5.

Few New Testament scholars support the findings of O'Callaghan and Thiede. At least three arguments have been advanced against their position, aside from the dispute over the *nu* in *autōn*. All objections appear to be from those outside the field of papyrology. The first argument concerns the problem created by the substitution of a *tau* where a *delta* should appear following the word *kai* in line three. Both Boismard (*editio princeps*) and O'Callaghan proposed that the letter *tau* follows the *kai*. Kurt Aland, and later, Vittoria Spottorno of the Spanish journal *Sefarad*, have identified *pi* as the letter following *kai*, but that identification appears to have been discounted. Though there are continuing arguments over what follows the *tau*,[197] an *iota* remains a

Editio princeps	O'Callaghan	Spottorno
].[	]ε.[	]τ[
]. τω α.. [	]υ.τωυ.η[	]εγωγε[
]η. και τω[	]η καιτι[	]σ καιπ[
ε. γε]ν□υησ.[ευ	]υ. υησ.[	]γυησ.[
]θ.ηε.σ.[	]θ.ησα.[	]ωηεγ[

strong possibility. Together, the *tau* and the *iota* begin the word *diaperasantes* with the *tau* replacing the *delta*.

Thiede has provided examples of a similar consonant shift in other literature of the period to explain the problem. For example, Josephus in his *Antiquities* (15.417) mentioned an inscription placed on the second wall of the Temple prohibiting entry to non-Jews on pain of death. This is the background for Acts 21:27-36 when Paul is threatened with death for allegedly bringing the non-Jew Trophimus into the Temple. One complete copy and one fragment of the inscription were found by archaeologists and the inscription had two spelling mistakes: in line one *medena* (nobody) is misspelled *methena*, and in line three *dryphakton* (barrier stone) was misspelled *tryphakton*. Thiede points out that the scribes had a problem with the soft *delta* and the misspelling of *dryphakton*, which is similar to the misspelling of *diaperasantes*, reflects the way Greek speaking Jews pronounced the *delta* in the Second Temple period. It would have been easy to mistake a *tau* for a *delta* because both consonants are articulated the same way and sound very much alike, with the difference that the *delta* is voiced.[198]

The second argument against Markan identification of 7Q5 is the dependence upon a variant; the words *epi tēn gēn* (upon the land) appear to be missing. Failure to come up with any known texts which would have this variant of Mark would appear to weaken the argument for Markan identification. However, Thiede explained that an earlier version of Mark with the phrase missing would make sense in a pre-Jewish War setting.

During the Roman war against the Jews, the nearby town of Gennesaret was destroyed, so the text would have needed to be clarified in future copies to remind readers that there was once a town there. The text in question would read: "After having crossed over, they came to Gennesaret..." instead of how it reads in all other known texts of Mark: "After having crossed over upon the land, they came to Gennesaret..." The phrase "upon the land" clarifies that Gennesaret is a town. According to Thiede, the missing phrase further buttresses the claim that this copy of Mark was indeed written before the Jewish war.[199]

The third argument contends that the letters *nu nu eta sigma* could support alternative readings such as *egennēsen* which means "beget." In fact, this was the original proposal of Boismard in the *editio princeps*. It was

103

originally thought that 7Q5 was a genealogical text. The problem with this conclusion is that there are no known Greek texts with this configuration *in combination with the other identifiable letters in the fragment.* With the placement of the *kai* in line three, and the identification of the *nu* as the ending letter for *autōn* in line two, the text could ONLY be Mark 6:52-53 with this juxtaposition of letters according to an *Ibykus* computer search of known texts.[200]

Spottorno claims the text is actually Zechariah 7:4-5. In the LXX version, line three would be reconstructed as *tēs gēs kai pros* (the...of the land and to...) from verse five, but what would the *epsilon gamma omega gamma epsilon* in line two correspond to? The only thing this author can surmise is *egeneto* (came) which does not fit her reconstruction. Also, Spottorno's reconstruction does not account for the space before the *kai* in line three. This and other forensic evidence detailed by Thiede rules out Spottorno's reconstruction.

Why so much emotion over this fragment? Why was O'Callaghan's proposal that 7Q5 was Mark 6:52-53 initially greeted with unenthusiastic silence and then, following additional support from papyrologist Herbert Hunger, attacked with such vehemence? The reason can be found in Muro's sarcastic remark concerning the mark below the alleged *nu* in line two being insect residue:

> "The question remains: What is that dark spot in the photograph of Thiede's *nu*? The humor that follows is inescapable: Is it a trace of writing that will demolish two centuries of higher critical scholarship, or is it simply poopie?"[201]

A possible conclusion might be that O'Callaghan and Thiede could not possibly be correct because it would put the authorship of Mark within the reasonable lifetime of an eyewitness and would question the idea that New Testament form critics know better than Ireneaus, Papias and other early church testimony which claims of eyewitness authorship of Scripture. Both conservative Bible scholars and more liberal scholars operate from opposing *a priori*.

For theological conservatives, the operating assumption that we live in a universe of cause and effect in an OPEN system results in the assertion of a high view of Scripture and the understanding that problem texts can be reconciled. Texts which are matter-of-fact about the miraculous are not problematic. For liberals, the operating assumption that we live in a universe of cause and effect in a CLOSED system leads to a low view of Scripture, the understanding that the Bible is hopelessly inconsistent, and that the miraculous is impossible.

It may be that O'Callaghan and Thiede are wrong and that the bible scholars are right. In fact, Roman Catholic O'Callaghan's chief critic, Ernest Muro does not fit into the above liberal/conservative scenario. On his website, Muro clarifies that he is a theologically conservative Roman Catholic. He is not one who believes we live in a closed universe of cause and effect. Therefore, it is unclear what his motivations are other than a desire to do good scholarship. Nevertheless, he does appear to have a stake in defending the form/higher critical scholastic orthodoxy.

This author's old professor of Church History and Philosophical Apologetics, Dr. John Warwick Montgomery, once stated that doing history involves working with both facts and interpretation. As much as one might like, one cannot get away from interpretation because a mere arrangement of facts is in itself an interpretation. Instead, one must recognize that facts are like a foot and interpretation is like a shoe. One must find the shoe that best fits the foot. Those who would do textual research involving biblical documents must recognize when an assumption about the universe becomes seen as an unassailable operative *a priori* similar to the way mathematics is seen for physics.

We are living in an age when the "sure results of higher criticism" are not so sure. We used to think that Pontius Pilate was a figment of the early church's imagination until archaeological evidence proved otherwise. We also used to think that the New Testament writings were all products of orthodox church formulations to combat heterodox writings produced about the same time: the late second century. The discovery of the Ryland's fragment of John's gospel and its subsequent dating to 125 C.E. pushed the composition of the New Testament, in the eyes of more and more scholars, into the first century. We need to make sure that we use the shoe that best fits the foot, so that we might have a better understanding of the momentous events of the first centuries B.C.E. and C.E. that have so shaped our own history and faith.

Index of Scripture

107

110

111

112

[1] Most scholars hold to this viewpoint. Some such as Lawrence Schiffman believe the group to be Sadducean. Others, such as Eisenman and Wise, propose them to be Jewish Christians; cf. Schiffman, Lawrence H. *"The Sadducean Origins of the Dead Sea Scroll Sect"* In *Understanding the Dead Sea Scrolls*. Edited by Hershel Shanks. New York: Vintage Books. 1993 and Eisenman, Robert and Michael Wise. *The Dead Sea Scrolls Uncovered*. New York: Penguin, 1992.

[2] In the July/August 1995 issue of *Biblical Archaeology Review* (Volume 21-Number 4) p. 61 there is a discussion of the most recent attempt at using Carbon-14 to date a text from the Qumran collection. The results found that there was a 68 per cent probability that the fragment was written between 35 B.C.E. and 59 C.E. and a 95 per cent probability that it was written between 93 B.C.E. and 80 C.E., confirming previous paleographic estimates. This would make it contemporary with or just before Jesus ministry and may reflect early sources for the gospels themselves. Of course, the accuracy of Carbon-14 dating can be disputed on the grounds of possible contamination (cf. Browne, Malcolm. "Errors Feared in Carbon Dating: Alternative Methods Used" *New York Times*, June 4, 1990). Other documents such as 4QMMT have been dated by concensus of scholars at 159 to 152 B.C.E. (Gillihan, Yonder Moynihan. *"Jewish Laws on Illicit Marriage, the Defilement of Offspring, and the Holiness of the Temple: A New Halakic Interpretation of 1 Corinthians 7:14"* In *Journal of Biblical Literature* 121:4, 2002, p. 721).

[3] Elwell, Walter A. and Robert W. Yarbrough. *Encountering the New Testament.* Grand Rapids, Michigan: Baker Academic. 2005, p. 172.

[4] Josephus, Flavius. *Antiquities of the Jews* 18:1, *Jewish War* 2:8; In Whiston, William (trans) *The Works of Flavius Josephus*. Grand Rapids, Michigan: Associated Publishers and Authors, pp. 377, 476-478.

[5] Betz, Otto. "Was John the Baptist an Essene?" In *Understanding the Dead Sea Scrolls*.

[6] Bruce, F. F. *The Canon of Scripture*. Downers Grove, Illinois: Inter-Varsity Press. 1988, pp. 117-133; if the gospels were edited, their final form appeared before the end of the first century C.E.

[7] Eusebius, *Ecclesiastical History*, 3.89.16. Eusebius references Papias' claims of a Hebrew/Aramaic original of Matthew's gospel (cf. Martin, Ralph P. *New Testament Foundations: A Guide for Christian Students*. v. 1. Grand Rapids, Michigan: Eerdmans. 1975, pp.238-240 for a discussion of various theories of authorship.)

[8] Eisenman and Wise, op. cit., p. 59

[9] "Torah" usually refers to the first five books of Moses. In this study, *tôrā* refers to the 613 laws taken from the entirety of the Hebrew Bible. "Breaking Torah" has come to signify the breaking of these laws.

[10] BDB p. 776. עָנָו noun. "poor, afflicted, humble, meek" (עָנָיו רק תָך).

[11] cf. Matthew 5:21, 27, 33, 38, 43. In Matthew 5:31 the variation Ἐρρέθη δε…ἐγὼ δὲ λέγω ὑμῖν is used.

[12] על...אנחנו אומרים cf. 4Q394f8c4:5, 4Q397f6c13:1,6; cf Garcia Martinez, Florentino. *The Dead Sea Scrolls Translated*. Wilfred G.E. Watson (trans). Grand Rapids, Michigan: Eerdmans, 1996, p. 82.

[13] "…applied to a person without education and devoid of morals (comp. Judges xi. 3)." Cf. Crawford Howell Toy and Jacob Zallel Lauterbach *Jewish Encylopedia.com* "*Raca/Reḳa*" <http://www.jewishencyclopedia.com/ view.jsp?artid=54&letter=R>

[14] Eisenman and Wise, op. cit., pp. 10, 11. Also, in Matthew 22:40 "hang"(κρεμάννυμι present passive indicative of κρέμαται) means "depend." Bertram in TDNT-3, p. 920 cites love as a "sustaining basis" in human conduct (cf. Romans 13:9, 10): "…the love of men for God is revealed and actualized in love for one's neighbor."

[15] Lohse, TDNT-9, pp. 682-683.

[16] BDB p. 446. Heb. יָשַׁע; Aramaic יתע.

[17] ביקדה רבתא ויושע אננון; Fitzmyer, Joseph A. *The Dead Sea Scrolls and Christian Origins*. Grand Rapids, Michigan: Eerdmans. 2000, p. 125.

[18] Ibid., pp. 124-125; The inscription at *Tell Fakhariyah* preserves "an effort to represent by the consonant *samekh* in the borrowed Phoenician alphabet the interdental ṯ (tha), which was still being so pronounced by the Arameans of this period." The Aramaic *yṯᶜ* is only used in proper names during this period. It is better known in a Hebrew guise as *yšᶜ*.

[19] Ibid, p. 187; מבקר.

[20] Ibid.

[21] Eisenman and Wise, op. cit., p. 217; García Martínez, op.cit., p. 44.

[22] BDB p. 1047. שָׁפַט verb. "judge, govern." Also, "decide controversy." This might be the equivalent of the deacons of the church in Christianity. Note the striking similarities between this description and a description of the appointment of certain men in Acts 6:1-5 as deacons to oversee the daily distribution of food.

[23] Garcia Martinez, op. cit., pp. 43-44.

[24] Fitzmyer, op. cit., p. 28.

[25] Banks, Robert. *Paul's Idea of Community.* Grand Rapids, Michigan: Eerdmans, 1980, pp. 34-46.

[26] Metzger, Bruce M. *A Textual Commentary on the Greek New Testament*. New York: United Bible Societies. 1975, p. 480. The United Bible Societies uses τὴν ἐκκλησίαν τοῦ θεου.

[27] הרבים or *hrbym* (vocalized *harabbim*) cf. Vanderkam, James. "The Dead Sea Scrolls and Christianity." In *Understanding the Dead Sea Scrolls*, p. 186.

[28] Ibid., p. 136.

[29] Foerster, TDNT-1, p. 607

[30] BDB p. 116. בְּלִיַּעַל noun. "worthlessness" (cpd. בְּלִי *not, without* and יַעַל *worth, use, profit*) -- the quality of "being useless, good for nothing."

[31] BDB p. 355, [חָרַם] verb. "ban, devote, exterminate" – "ban, devote (esp. religiously, sq. objects hostile to the theocracy; this involved gen. their destruction; when a city was

`devoted' the inhabitants were put to death, the spoil being destroyed or not acc. to the gravity of the occasion…)"

[32] BDB p. 393. יָדַע qal imperfect. Literally "know by experience." It is a euphemism for intimate relations. The men were planning sodomy and may have been induced through ritualized use of pornographic objects as part of idol worship.

[33] Vanderkam, op. cit., p. 188; cf also Fitzmyer, Joseph. "4Q Testimonia and the New Testament," *Theological Studies*, 18, 1957, pp. 534-535.

[34] BDB p. 364. מַחֲשָׁבָה noun. "thought, device" (chiefly poetic and late).

[35] Eisenman and Wise, op. cit., p. 224,

[36] BDB p. 558. מוּר verb. "change."

[37] Matthew 12:24-28 records an exchange between Jesus and the Pharisees in which Jesus is accused of doing miracles by Beelzebub (Baalzebub), an apparent synonym for Satan and similar in etymology to Belial.

[38] BDB p. 606; מֶמְשָׁלָה noun. "rule, dominion, realm."

[39] Garcia Martinez, op. cit., p. 280. The "rule" of these angels should be understood as "have dominion/power" as it is in Daniel 11:4 (cf. BDB p. 605. מָשַׁל vb. "rule, have dominion, reign" -- verb qal perfect 3rd person common plural. human subject, "rule, have dominion" over (בְ))

[40] BDB p. 966. Eisenman and Wise, op. cit., p. 54.

[41] מעשי התורה

[42] Lawrence H. Schiffman presents an excellent analysis of the Qumran sectarian literature and how it helps us to understand the pharisaic ancestry of modern rabbinic Judaism (cf. Schiffman, L. "New Light on the Pharisees" In *Understanding the Dead Sea Scrolls*. Edited by Hershel Shanks. New York: Vintage Books. 1993).

[43] שמי מהם⁶ וה○] -- . ○[זכור את מלכי ישראנ̇ל] והתבנן במעשיהמ̇ה
שהיא יראנ̇ את -- התחזרה היה מצולן]מצרות

[44] Generally, I am following the text supplied by Florentino García Martínez. However, Eisenman and Wise translate חשב as "reckon" which is possible. This would be reminiscent of Paul's language in Romans and Galatians.

[45] ונחשבה לך לצדקה The Niphal Perfect of חָשַׁב suggests a completed action done to oneself. (cf. LaSor, William Sanford. *Handbook of Biblical Hebrew, Vol. 2*. Grand Rapids, Michigan: Eerdmans. 1979, pp. 106, 157, 167; BDB p. 363).

[46] ויצדקו והלך על הר○ם. Garcia Martinez, op. cit., p. 228. Eisenman and Wise (p. 49) mistranslate the text to say "they were justified, and walked according to the Laws" because they did not have an accurate copy.

[47] Longenecker, Richard N. *"The Acts of the Apostles"* In *The Expositor's Bible Commentary*. Edited by Frank E. Gaebelein. Grand Rapids, Michigan: Zondervan. 1981, p. 333, and Joachim Jeremias. *Jerusalem in the Time of Jesus.* Translated by F. H. and C.H. Cave. Philadelphia: Fortress. 1969, pp. 198-213.

[48] Longenecker, op. cit., p. 446.

[49] Haenchen, Ernst. *The Acts of the Apostles*. Translated by R. McL. Wilson. Philadelphia: Westminster, 1971, p. 448.

[50] 4Q174, also know as 4QFlorilegium, has the text from Amos 9:11 read הנופלת והקימותי את סוכת דויד "I will raise up the hut (booth) of David which has fallen." This is almost identical to the LXX and the text used in Acts 15 which has ἀναστήσω τὴν σκηνὴν Δαυιδ τὴν πεπτωκυῖαν. The Masoretic text has דָּוִיד הַנֹּפֶלֶת אָקִים אֶת־סֻכַּת.

[51] The Hebrew text of Amos found in Qumran Cave Four and Wâdi Murabbaᶜat is incomplete and appears to follow the MT (c.f. Abegg, Martin, Peter Flint and Eugene Ulrich. *The Dead Sea Scrolls Bible.* San Francisco: HarperCollins. 1999, p. 440).

[52] Longenecker, R. N., op. cit., p. 459.

[53] Garcia Martinez, op. cit., p. 79 has "in justice" here, but I think it is clearer to translate לצדקה as "righteousness" or "justification" (literally, "toward righteousness"). לפניו ונחשבה לך לצדקה בעֲשֹׁותְךָ הישר

[54] The Ebionites, a sect known at least from the time of Irenaeus, denied the deity of Jesus, believed in keeping the entire Law of Moses including circumcision, used only a Hebrew gospel of Matthew, and scorned Paul (cf. Eusebius, *Ecclesiastical History*, 3:27). They were the natural inheritors of the point of view of the Judaizers who were marginalized after the first church council in Galatians 2 and Acts 15. Berkhof claims the Ebionites were Pharisaic in origin; however, their name means "the poor" in Hebrew and given that this was often a designation that the Qumran community gave itself (cf. Eisenman and Wise, op. cit., pp. 233-234; 1QH, 4Q299, 4Q416, 4Q418, 4Q434, 4Q437 to name just a few) it is more likely that the Judaizers, and ultimately, the Ebionites came from them (cf. Berkhof, Louis. *The History of Christian Doctrines*. Grand Rapids, Michigan: Baker. 1975, p. 44; Latourette, Kenneth Scott. *A History of Christianity*, Vol. 1. San Francisco: Harper. 1975, p.p. 121-122).

[55] It is well-known that many in the Messianic movement look forward to a rebuilding of the Temple in Jerusalem so they can resume sacrifices. This would parallel the Qumran documents' zeal for a purified Temple, not the one controlled by the Sadducees (see also Eisenmen and Wise, op.cit., pp. 185-186).

[56] Crossan, John Dominic and Jonathan L. Reed. *Excavating Jesus*. San Francisco: Harpers. 2001, pp. 167-171.

[57] *Kelim 10:1*

[58] BDB, p. 619; נָגַע בְּרֹשׁ verb. "to strike"

[59] טמאות האדם If ancient writers are correct in that the Essenes, in general, were unmarried males, and if the Qumran community were Essenes following this social structure, then the phrase would be a reference to masturbation or nocturnal emissions.

[60] שְׁכְבַת־זָרַע "a layer of dew" (i.e., emission of semen).

[61] Dunn, James D. G. *New Testament Studies* 48, 2002, p. 451; cf. Sanders, E. P. *Jesus and Judaism*. London: SCM, 1985, pp. 182-183.

[62] Rudolph, David J. "Yeshua and the Dietary Laws: A Reassessment of Mark 7:19a" In *Kesher: A Journal of Messianic Judaism.* (Issue 16, Fall 2003), pp. 97-119. The author argues for the continuation of kosher regulations into the present covenant for Jews. He apparently misunderstands that the "Gentile exemption from the Leviticus 11 dietary laws" is a *de facto* exemption for all those in the New Covenant as this New Covenant changes everything.

[63] Longenecker, op. cit., p. 387.

[64] BDB p. 158 גֵּר noun. "a sojourner, temporary dweller, or new-comer"

[65] BDB p. 850 צָחַק verb. "to laugh" This verb is the root word for "Issac" and means to toy with or make sport. It can also mean to caress with sexual overtones as in Genesis 26:8.

[66] Josephus, Flavius. 2:17:2. *The Great Roman-Jewish War*. Trans. by William Whiston. Mineola, New York: Dover Publications. 2004, p. 145.

[67] Ibid., pp. 80, 81, and 83.

[68] Ibid., pp. 47-49.

[69] García Martínez, op.cit., p. 228.

[70] Pastor Jon Courson also infers as much and even gives us an imaginative possible exchange between Balak and Balaam on the matter (cf. Courson. *A Day's Journey*. Santa Ana, California: Calvary Chapel Publishing. 2003, pp. 258-259).

[71] Fitzmyer, op. cit., pp. 79-82.

[72] Ibid, p. 82-107, and Burrows, Millar. *The Dead Sea Scrolls.* New York: Viking Press. 1956, p. 330; for a maverick viewpoint, see Eisenman and Wise, op. cit., p. 85.

[73] Fitzmyer, op. cit., p. 83.

[74] Ibid., pp. 78-79.

[75] García Martínez, op.cit., pp. 13-14; עד בוא נביא ומשיחי אהרון וישראל

[76] Ibid., p. 127; יוליד [אל [א]נֿת]המשיח אתם

[77] Ibid., p. 13.

[78] BDB p. 458. כָּבוֹד.

[79] García Martínez, op.cit., p. 394; "revive the dead" in Fitzmyer, op. cit., p. 94-95; ומתים יחיה; Eisenman and Wise translate the phrase "resurrect the dead" (p. 23) and go on to say "this is the first definitive reference to resurrection in the corpus (p. 21)."

[80] Eisenman and Wise, op. cit., p. 19.

[81] BDB, p. 339. חֶסֶד.

[82] ולנֿע]לם אדבק [בבמֿ]יֿחלים ובחסדו יֿן [cf. Eisenman and Wise, op. cit., p. 23 and García Martínez, op. cit., p. 394 for more established translations.

[83] BDB pp. 1033-1034. שָׁמַע

[84] יעשה אדני כאשר דֿנבר] כֿי ירפא חללים ומתים יחיה ענוים יבשר ונכבֿדות שלוא היו . cf. Eisenman and Wise, op. cit., p. 23 and Florentino Garcia Marinez, op. cit., p. 394 for more established translations.

[85] BDB p. 776. עָנָו noun. "poor, afflicted, humble, meek" (עָנִיו) – (a) "poor, needy" (Qr). (b) "poor and weak," oppressed by rich and powerful (c) "poor, weak and afflicted" Israel (usu. rendered *meek*). (d) "humble, lowly, meek"

[86] Ibid, p. 20; cf. Josephus. *Jewish Wars* II.8.10 and *Antiquities of the Jews* XV.10.4.

[87] Since Melchizedek means "king of righteousness," presumably the "men of the lot of Melchizedek" are those who are ruled by righteousness. However, later in the document, Melchizedek himself is a divine being who frees from the hand of Belial.

[88] BDB 497. כֹּפֶר noun. "the price of a life, ransom."

[89] García Martínez, op.cit., p. 35.

[90] Ibid., p. 86.

[91] Ibid., p. 414.

[92] Brown, Colin. "*Reconciliation*" NIDNTT 3, p. 151-160; see also Hammond, T. C. *In Understanding Be Men*. Downers Grove, Illinois: Inter-Varsity Press. 1968, pp. 119-121.

[93] Fitzmyer, op. cit., pp. 38-39.

[94] The prophecy of the 70 weeks of years begins with the decree of Cyrus in 538 B.C.E. and ends with the arrival of Jesus in Jerusalem in April of 31 AD. One week still remains.

[95] Abegg, Flint and Ulrich, op. cit., p. 484.

[96] Fitzmyer, op. cit., p. 32.

[97] Ibid, p. 70; García Martínez, op. cit., p. 138.

[98] Fitzmyer argues that this "Son of God" is speaking of some coming ruler who may be a successor of David but is not the Messiah. His views would be in line with Old Testament understanding of messiah, but not first century C.E. understanding. The point is not what the Old Testament writers understood about the Messiah but what the first century Jews expected. He seems to come to his conclusion because the word *māšîăh*☐ was not found in the text. Fitzmyer admits that the text proves that the terms "Son of God" and "Son of the Most High" were not alien to Palestinian Judaism. From the text we know that he is at least a ruler and his kingdom is everlasting. We also know from 4Q252 that the Messiah will be a descendent of David. It seems to me that this is enough to demonstrate the terms are interchangeable.

[99] Fitzmyer, op. cit., p. 50; cf. Mark 15:34 ελωι ελωι λεμα σαβαχθανι; ὅ ἐστιν μεθερμηνευόμενον· ὁ θεός μου ὁ θεός μου, εἰς τί ἐγκατέλιπές με; Psalm 21:2 (LXX) ὁ θεὸς ὁ θεός μου πρόσχες μοι ἵνα τί ἐγκατέλιπές με ; Psalm 22:2 (MT) לָמָה עֲזַבְתָּנִי אֵלִי אֵלִי.

[100] 4Q4252 c 6 5:3-4 עד בוא משיח הצדק צמח דויד cf. Eisenman and Wise, op. cit., p. 89; García Martínez, op. cit., p. 215.

[101] Pagels, Elaine. *Beyond Belief*. New York: Random House. 2003, pp. 37-38. In fact, the date for the final composition of Mark, whom she uses as a benchmark for identifying Jewish messianic expectations (pp. 38, 45), was probably even earlier than 68-70 C.E..

[102] Oepke, A. TDNT-4, p. 599.

[103] Moses, as a supplicant intercessor between God and Israel (Exodus 32:30-35 and Numbers 14:11-20); Abraham ,as intercessor (Genesis 18:23-33); the prophets, as an intermediary-intercessor (Isaiah 59:16).

[104] Oepke, A. TDNT-4, p. 619.

[105] Missler, Chuck. *"Textual Controversy: Mischievous Angels or Sethites?"* **Personal Update NewsJournal.** August 1997.

[106] Eisenman and Wise, op. cit., p. 95. The Bible designation in Genesis and Job for "sons of God" is בְּנֵ הָאֱלֹהִים.

[107] Hendel, Ronald S. "When the Sons of God Cavorted with the Daughters of Men." In **Understanding the Dead Sea Scrolls.** New York: Random House. 1993, p. 173; cf. BDB p. 657 נָפַל Esp. of violent death (+ שָׁדוּד); + וַיְמָת, etc.; נ' חָלָל fall pierced (fatally);" חַלְלֵי חֶרֶב; cf. נ' פְּגָרִים בְּתוֹךְ חֲלָלִים; "corpses fall;" by the sword, בְּחֶרֶב; בְּיַד "by the hand of;" תַּחַת נ' רַגְלַי *fall under my feet*; Jeremiah 6:15, 9:22.

[108] cf. The Catholic Encyclopedia <http://www.newadvent.org/cathen/08565a.htm> and Crosswalk.com. <http://www.biblestudytools.net/History/AD/EarlyChurchFathers/Ante-Nicene/JuliusAfricanus/>.

[109] The word οἰκητήριον simply means "dwelling" or "home."

[110] Chang, Julia. **Confucianism and Christianity.** Tokyo: Kodansha International.1977, p. 20; cf also Legge, James (ed.) **The Four Books.** Taibei, Taiwan: Culture Book Company, for examples of the use of *shang di* by Confucius.

[111] Montgomery, John W., ed. **God's Inerrant Word.** Minneapolis, Minnesota: Bethany Fellowship. 1974, pp. 278-279.

[112] This is, of course, an admission of an *a priori* with regard to forming a hermeneutic. However, due to the absence of human omniscience, we understand that everyone must operate under an *a priori*. The question then becomes, "Which *a priori* best operates within the facts?" One should always be prepared to abandon an *a priori* if the facts warrant.

[113] Bietenhard, H. NIDNTT v. 1, p. 101.

[114] Von Rad, TDNT v. 1, p. 78. See especially note 19.

[115] In Leviticus 10, Aaron is exhorted by God, under threat of death, not to drink wine before entering the holy place as he is to make a distinction between the holy and the common. This is reiterated in Ezekiel's complaint against the priests; cf . TWOT 2, p. 787.

[116] υριάσιν Καδης ἐκ δεξιῶν αὐτοῦ ἄγγελοι μετ' αὐτοῦ

[117] חֶבֶל "ruin" Micah 2:10. Often used to refer to the pains of childbirth. Isaiah 26:17; also "snares" Job 21:17.

[118] Wise, M, M. Abegg, E. Cook. "The Dead Sea Scrolls." San Francisco: Harper. 2005, p. 417; 'ābôt "forefather" "father" "ancestor' "family" Joshua 22:14, 1 Kings 8:1.

[119] שָׁבוּעַ unit (period) of seven, seven days, a week Daniel 9:27.

[120] מֶמְשָׁלָה realm or territory of one's authority; dominion, realm 1 Kings 9:19, 2 Kings 20:13, Pslams 114:5.

[121] שְׁעָרָיו שַׁעַר "the gates of heaven" Genesis 28:17, Psalm 100:4; cf. "gates of the camp" Exodus 32:26 , "gates of a courtyard" Exodus 27:16. A place where the business or government of the city is conducted. Psalm 69:12, Proverbs 22:22; 24:7.

[122] שַׁחַת :שָׁחַת, שִׁחְתָם; (1) "a pit" (to trap animals) Ezekiel 19:4 (2) "pit, grave" (abode of the dead = Sheol) Psalm 103:4; Isa. 38:17 (BDB p. 1007)

[123] ומשאול אבדון . פדיתה נפשי משחת "you have redeemed my soul from pit, from Sheol and Abaddon." (cf. Wise, Abegg, and Cook, op. cit., p. 182).

[124] מִשְׁפָּט Psalm 36:7 a legal decision, justice, righteousness, cf. Jeremiah 32:8

[125] נָשִׂי נָשִׂיא; cs. נְשִׂיא; pl. נְשִׂ(י)אִים, cs. נְשִׂיאֵי: "chief, minor king": Abraham Genesis 23:6; in family of Ishmael Genesis 17:20, and foreign tribes, e.g. Midian Numbers 25:18, but usually in Israel leader of a given tribe of Numbers 2 (BDB 672).

[126] טוהר o[רזי יודעי לנכו]לן "observe the mysteries of purity" probably having to do without bodily imperfections (Leviticus 12:4; 2 Kings 5:10).

[127] תמימי דרך "honest/blameless journey" Genesis 6:9, Psalm 119:1

[128] The Aramaic text seems to suggest "holy ones"; cf. Wise, Abegg, and Cook, op. cit., p. 541.

[129] עִיר "one who is awake; watcher" Daniel

[130] קַדִּישִׁין אֱלָהִין רוּחַ varient קַדִּישׁ Heb. קָדוֹשׁ: "Holy One" or God; pl. קַדִּישִׁין, cs. קַדִּישֵׁי; " holy gods" Daniel 4:5-15; 5:11; n. "angels"

[131] Charles, R.H. *The Apocrypha and Pseudepigrapha of the Old Testament.* Oxford: Claredon, 1912. <http://www.heaven.net.nz/writings/thebookofenoch.htm>; cf. Martinez, op. cit., p. 256

[132] Ibid.

[133] Charles, Ibid.; Martinez, op. cit., p. 258

[134] Eisenman and Wise, op. cit., p. 95

[135] כעיוין Wise, Abegg, and Cook, op.cit., p. 540

[136] צדק[מלוכי]גורל]אנשי[ו]אור [אור בני The word for "God" is not in the text but is inferred from the context. It is probably a reference to "sons of God" in Job, in which case, these would be heavenly beings (cf, 11Q13:14 אל בְּנֵי also, Chapter Four).

[137] Weiss, K. TDNT-6, p. 958. Weiss says that the origin of fever is supernatural, either as divine punishment or demonic attack.

[138] εἰς διαταγὰς ἀγγέλων God directed the angels to transmit the Law (BAG, p. 188).

[139] διαταγεὶς δι' ἀγγέλων ἐν χειρὶ μεσίτου. According to Moule, Galatians 3:19 is a pure Hebraism "and should not be translated into English by any phrase containing the word hand." Moule, C.F.D. *Idiom Book of New Testament Greek.* Cambridge University Press: Cambridge. 1977, p. 184.

[140] Grundman, TDNT 1, p. 76.

[141] Mare, W. Harold. *The Expositor's Bible Commentary*, **Vol. 10**, p. 255 suggests that *katakaluptō* could mean "put up" because in the ancient world, letting the hair hang down would be understood as "the shame of an accused adultress."

[142] God comes with the clouds in judgment. Zephaniah 1:15, 16 says that God will come with the clouds (angels), darkness and a trumpet; cf. Ezekiel 30:3, 32:7 and Joel 2:2. See also, Exodus 19:9, 16; 24:15-16, 18; Deuteronomy 4:11, 5:22 and Psalms 97:2.

[143] The same could be said for the line in Genesis 10:14: אֲשֶׁר יָצְאוּ מִשָּׁם פְּלִשְׁתִּים which would have the Philistines come out of the Casluhites. 1 Chronicles 1:11 follows Genesis 10:14, but Amos 9:7 claims that the Philistines came from the Caphtorites. The line is an explanatory gloss based on the Amos text that a latter scribe copied into the Genesis 10:14 text in the wrong place (cf. Wurthwein, Ernst. *The Text of the Old Testament*. Grand Rapids, Eerdmans. 1995). Eisenman and Wise (p. 268) note that archaeological evidence suggests that the Philistines should actually be sons of Japhet and identified with the Kittîm, though no citation to back this up is provided.

[144] BDB p. 508. כִּתִּיִּים noun proper no gender no number no state; [כִּתִּי] adjective, always plural.; usually as noun "Cypriotes;" כִּתִּים (as son of Yawan); וְצִים מִיַּד כ' "ships from the side (direction) of Kittîm;" more generally, of coast-lands of Mediterranean; even of Macedonian Greece, צִיִּים כִּתִּים i.e. "Grecian ships."

[145] BDB p. 986. שֵׁבֶט noun **(a)** "rod, staff, club, scepter." **(b)** "tribe."

[146] García Martínez, op.cit., p. 195.

[147] [--]°כתיים [מל'ن]כ[--] [--]בני לוי ועם הארץ[--] [--]בֹּני לוי ועם הארץ[--] מלך יהודה [ויגלה --] [--] צד]קיה -- (4Q247 f1:4-6).

[148] Vaughan, Curtis. "Colossians." *The Expositor's Bible Commentary, v. 11*, p. 198; στοιχεἰα, ων n can refer to elements (physical building blocks such as atoms) or "elemental spirits" (with supernatural powers used to coerce men).

[149] Goulder, Michael. "Hebrews and the Ebionites." *New Testament Studies* 49. 2003, p. 393.

[150] Ibid., p. 395.

[151] Irenaeus, *Adversus Haereses* 1.26.2.

[152] Eisenman and Wise, op. cit., pp. 106-107.

[153] Ibid., p. 108; BDB p. 1038. מִשְׁמֶרֶת means "guard, watch," also "charge, function." It is found in descriptions of the priestly duties (cf. Numbers 3:7).

[154] Eisenman and Wise, op. cit., pp. 106-109.

[155] Ibid, p. 258.

[156] BDB, p. 890. קָסַם vb. denom. "practice divination" **1.**"of diviners of the nations," e.g. "Balaam, Philistines." cf. ק' שׁוא; (1) "of Cannanite necromancers; of Ammonites. (2) false proph. of Isr. **3.** ק' קְסָמִים prohibited."

[157] Flavius Josephus, *Jewish War*, 5.217-18, in Flavius Josephus, Complete Works, 9 Vols., trans. H. St. John Thackeray, III (Loeb Classical Library: Cambridge: Harvard University Press; London: William Heinemann, 1926-63), pp. 266-67.

[158] Eisenman and Wise, op. cit., p. 116.

[159] Glueck, Nelson. *Hesed in the Bible*. Translated by Alfred Gottschalk. Hebrew University Press. 1967.

[160] BDB p. 338. חֶסֶד noun. "goodness, kindness." **I.** *of man*: *kindness* of men towards men, in doing favours and benefits. **II.** of God: kindness, lovingkindness" in condescending to the needs of his creatures. He is חַסְדָּם "their goodness, favour." (1) specifically lovingkindness: (a) "in redemption from enemies and troubles;" men should trust in it; rejoice in it; hope in it. (b) "in preservation of life from death. (c) in quickening of spiritual life." (d) in redemption from sin. (e) in keeping the covenants," with Abraham; with Moses and Israel; with David and his dynasty; with the wife Zion. (2) חֶסֶד is grouped with other divine attributes: חסד ואמת "kindness (lovingkindness) and fidelity."

[161] BDB p. 145. גָּאַל "kinsman." (a) in taking a kinsman's widow. (b) in redeeming from bondage; (c) in redeeming a field; (d) claim as kinsman; the Dead Sea Scrolls 4Q185 f1_2ii:10 ; 4Q381 f24a+b:5 "save, redeem."

[162] שִׂים־נָא יָדְךָ תַּחַת יְרֵכִי "put your hand under my thigh" The servant was to place hand on the penis (cf. Genesis 46:26, Exodus 1:5).

[163] Eichrodt, Walthur. *Theology of the Old Testament*. V. 1.Trans. by J.A. Baker. Philadelphia: Westminster Press. 1961, p. 37; cf. LaRue, Gerald. Introduction to *Hesed in the Bible*. Glueck, op. cit., pp. 6-7.

[164] Eichrodt, op. cit., p. 38.

[165] Bultmann, R. TDNT-2, p. 477 "In Greek, ἔλεος is a παθός, i.e., the emotion roused by contact with an affliction which comes undeservedly on someone else." ἐλεήμων and πολυέλεος are related to ἔλεος.

[166] Bruce, F. F. op. cit., p. 40.

[167] Cross, op. cit., p. 155.

[168] *Babylonian Talmud*. Edited and translated by I. Epstein. London: Soncino Press. 1948. Tractate *Baba Bathra* Folio 14b-15a <http://www.come-and-hear.com/bababathra/bababathra_14.html#PARTb ><http://www.come-and-hear.com/bababathra/bababathra_15.html>

[169] Cf. Luke 24:27-32, 45, John 5:39, Acts 17:2, 11, 18:24-28, Romans 1:2, 15:4, 1 Corinthians 3, 4, and 2 Timothy 3:15.

[170] Bruce, F. F., op. cit., p. 31.

[171] The addition in Matthew 24:35 of "son of Barachiah" is probably a scribal gloss.

[172] Cf. Romans 9:13 (Malachi 1:2,3); Romans 11:8 (1 Kings 9:18); Romans 11:26 (Isaiah 59:20-21, 27:9, Jeremiah 31:33, 34); Romans 15:9-12 (2 Samuel 22:50, Psalm 18:40, Deuteronomy 32:43, Psalm 117:1, Isaiah 11:10); 1 Corinthians 3:19 (Job 5:13); and Galatians 3:10 (Deuteronomy 27:26, Habukkuk 2:4, Leviticus 18:5). Of course, many Old Testament books were quoted in this manner many times over, especially Deuteronomy, Psalms, and Isaiah.

[173] BDB p. 706. שֶׁפֶר

[174] The Roman Catholic Church regards Tobit as deutero-canonical.

[175] Cf. Colley, Caleb. *Did Jude Treat Noncanonical Writings as if They Were Inspired?* Apolegetics Press. 2004. <http://www.apologeticspress.org/articles/2235>; Bruce, F. F., op. cit., p. 51.

[176] Bruce, F. F.,op. cit., p. 49.

[177] Ibid.

[178] Abegg, Flint, and Ulrich, op.cit., p. xvii.

[179] Cross, op. cit., pp. 146, 154-155.

[180] Stegemann, Hartmut. "*Is the Temple Scroll a Sixth Book of the Torah—Lost for 2,500 Years?*" *Understanding the Dead Sea Scrolls*.

[181] 1QpHab 11:9 has שתה גם אתה והרעל whereas, the MT has גַּם־אַתָּה וְהֵעָרֵל שְׁתֵה; cf. García Martínez, op. cit., p. 202.

[182] Eisenman and Wise, op. cit., p. 76.

[183] Ibid., p. 76.

[184] García Martínez, op.cit., p. 220.

[185] Abegg, Flint and Ulrich, op. cit., p. 156.

[186] Shea, William H. "*The Structure of the Genesis Flood Narrative and Its Implications.*" Geoscience Research Institute. 1979. <http://www.grisda.org/origins/06008.htm>

[187] Ibid., pp. 81-84.

[188] BDB p. 31. "The *end* or ultimate *issue* of a course of action; of a prediction" the event: *Isaiah 41:22.* בְּאַחֲרִית הַיָּמִים "in the end of the days," a prophetic phrase denoting the final period of the history so far as the speaker's perspective reaches; the sense thus varies with the context, but it often = the ideal or Messianic future."

[189] Evans, Craig A. "*How Septuagintal is Isa. 5:1-7 in Mark 12:1-9?*" in *Novum Testamentum* XLV, 2. Koninklijke Brill NV, Leiden, 2003, pp. 105-110.

[190] Abegg, Flint and Ulrich, op. cit., p. 277.

[191] Gillihan, op.cit., pp. 711-744.

[192] Ibid, p. 713.

[193] Fitzmyer, op. cit., p. 24.

[194] Thiede, Carsten P. *Greek Qumran Fragment 7Q5: Possibilities and Impossibilities.* The Donaldson Corporation, 2005. <http://members.aol.com/egweimi/7q5.htm>

[195] Muro, Ernest A., Jr. *No Nu on Line 2, Part 1: Is the Definitive Dark Spot on Carsten Peter Thiede's High-Resolution Photograph a Trace of Writing, or is it a Poopie?* March 2003. <http://www.breadofangels.com/dssresources/7q5line2/nonu1.html>

[196] Muro, Ernest A., Jr. *No Nu on Line 2, Part 2a: An Evaluation of the Papyrological Evidence versus the Claims of Carsten Peter Thiede in the Dead Sea Scrolls and the Jewish Origins of Christianity.* September, 2003. <http://www.breadofangels.com/dssresources/7q5line2/nonu2.html>

[197] The *editio princeps* identifies an *omega* following the *tau*, and Muro (7Q5: *Disloqué à Droite, Key to the Controversy* 2001 <http://www.breadofangels.com/7q5/key.html>) argues for an *omega* or a *sigma*.

[198] Thiede, Carsten Peter and Matthew D'Ancona. ***Eyewitness to Jesus: Amazing New Manuscript Evidence About the Origin of the Gospels***. New York: Doubleday. 1996, pp. 31-37.

[199] Ibid, p. 38.

[200] Thiede, Carsten P. *Greek Qumran Fragment 7Q5: Possibilities and Impossibilities.* The Donaldson Corporation, 2005 <http://members.aol.com/egweimi/7q5.htm>

[201] Muro, Ernest A., Jr. No Nu on Line 2, Part 1: *Is the Definitive Dark Spot on Carsten Peter Thiede's High-Resolution Photograph a Trace of Writing, or is it a Poopie?* March 2003.

www.ingramcontent.com/pod-product-compliance
Lightning Source LLC
Chambersburg PA
CBHW031859090426
42741CB00005B/564